The Best Of
Children's Product Design

The Best Of
Children's Product Design

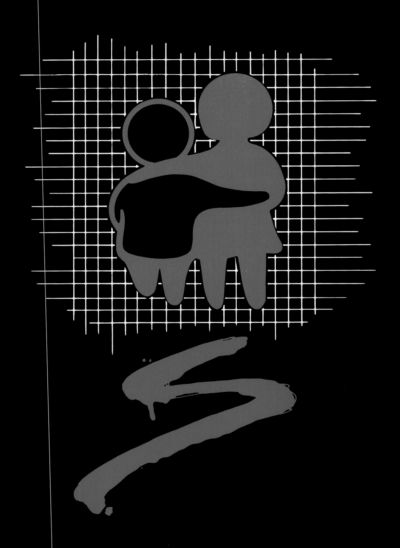

By Stewart Mosberg and the editors of

PBC International, Inc. ■ New York

Distributor to the book trade in the United
States and Canada:
Rizzoli International Publications, Inc.
597 Fifth Avenue
New York, NY 10017

Distributor to the art trade in the United
States:
Letraset USA
40 Eisenhower Drive
Paramus, NJ 07653

Distributed throughout the rest of the
world by:
Hearst Books International
105 Madison Avenue
New York, NY 10016

Library of Congress Cataloging-in-Publication Data

Mosberg, Stewart.
    The best of children's product design / by
Stewart Mosberg and the editors of PBC International.
        p.   cm.
    Includes indexes.
    ISBN 0-86636-067-0 : $55.00
    1. Design, Industrial. 2. Children's   paraphernailia.
    I. PBC.
International.   II Title.
TS171.4.M68   1988
745.2–dc 19   88-60878
                                                CIP

Color separation, printing and binding by
Toppan Printing Co. (H.K.) Ltd. Hong Kong

Typography by RMP Publication Services

10 9 8 7 6 5 4 3 2 1

STAFF

MANAGING DIRECTOR	Penny Sibal-Samonte
CREATIVE DIRECTOR	Richard Liu
FINANCIAL DIRECTOR	Pamela McCormick
ASSOCIATE ART DIRECTOR	Daniel Kouw
EDITORIAL MANAGER	Kevin Clark
ARTISTS	William Mack
	Kim McCormick

Contents

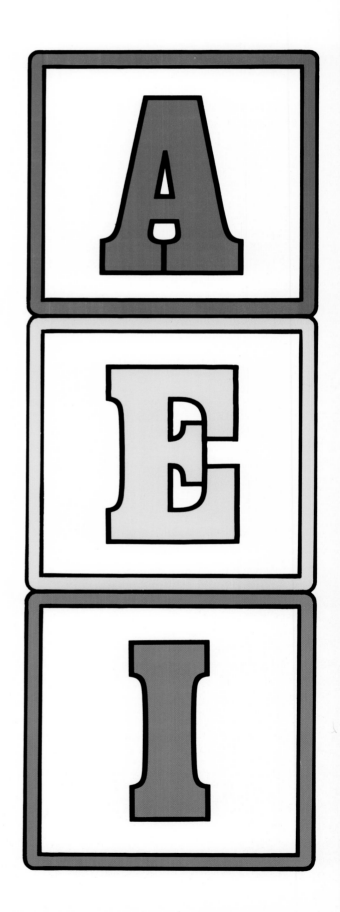

in children's design, Mom may hate hot pink.

Testing children and mothers has also shown that simplicity in design is important. Parents are reluctant to buy their preschoolers a product with lots of parts. The exceptions are play sets with storage areas and construction sets. Storage is important for clean up, and good basic play value is important to the preschooler.

Another major factor is safety. When designing clothes, for example, parents are concerned with durability, fire resistance and toxicity. All fabrics should be tested for fire retardance, toxic dyes, durability and safety when put in the mouth. Plush, for example, could be dangerous if the fur comes out during or after it has been chewed.

Through observation of children playing with toys, we have discovered the importance of eliminating pinch points. Any opening, such as the wheel well on a toy truck, should be one-quarter of an inch away from the tire. Any less can cause a nasty pinch to a little finger. Swallow size for small parts must also be considered, and the length of a cord is important to prevent choking.

Besides safety, ease of use is also an important factor. For example, velcro on clothing has become an excellent way for young children to begin dressing themselves without the age-old button problem.

Where the product will be marketed and to whom is the next major factor. Will the product be advertised through television advertising and directed at children or will advertising be directed at parents through magazines? At this point, I always work closely with my client's marketing department for as much information as I can get about the product's marketing program. For example, if we are working on a baby rattle for a three-

month-old we will design the product for the baby and the package for the parent. For baby, we must consider safety, size, color, toxicity, motor control and the product's overall quality. For the parent, all of these factors are important, but we must first get his or her attention at the marketplace.

Recently we designed a line of video boxes for children from three years of age and up to be marketed for a major Japanese company in video stores throughout the United States. Our design focus on the package had to be appealing to the parent, fall into the video store marketing trends, and yet look like a children's product.

Our approach was to understand the video market for young children by examining the juvenile book market, because of the familiarity they have with books. After much research and preliminary concept work, we decided on a booklike approach with our package design. Our reasoning was that the parent was also familiar with the books and such a design would take a bit of the confusion out of the purchase in the video stores with thousands of the same size packages. The color and graphics were designed with the ultimate consumer in mind—the child.

In the publishing field we must deal with other design factors including type size, language, color, and, most importantly, art style. For preschoolers under age five there is a feel of art style that the parent and children enjoy. We might call it a fun, or cartoon look. However, if these books are to be used in schools we must be careful of state regulations on art standards. For example, showing an animal with clothes on may be taboo. And, in New York and other states you need an ethnic balance, which is usually 60 percent western European

and 40 percent non-western. Of the 40 percent, 15 percent are Black, 13 percent are Hispanic, 10 percent are Asian, and 2 percent all others. When doing any designing for children you must know the law and current standards, especially in the public school industry when it comes to what will be in a classroom.

Other factors to consider in marketing are licensed characters and older children. The popularity of such licensed characters as Mickey Mouse on a product or fashion will play a major role in the purchase by the parent as well as in the preschooler's enjoyment. The characters seen on television and in books become a part of a child's everyday life. Marketing departments usually have the latest information on which characters are the hottest for that year. Older children, age 6 to 16, also play a part in the world of design for preschoolers by their their visual look as well as through the preschoolers' interest in emulating what older children eat, drink, wear, watch on television, listen to in music and play with in toys.

The market has expanded to such an extent that there are now major trade magazines that specialize in children's marketing for fashions, accessories, toys, videos and so on!

Designing for children is involved. There are many major factors that must be considered in a good, safe design, at both the marketing and the retail level, as well as in what the child will enjoy.

Introduction

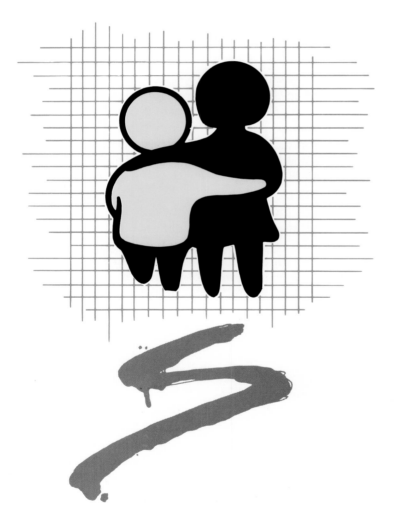

Human beings, in their capacity to reason, know few things in life are guaranteed. The knowledge of this comes from experience; our own and that of our ancestors.

One *is* certain, however—if you're reading this, you were a child once or you are one now.

The promise held out to us as children is at once fascinating and challenging.

Designing for children holds the same promise for adults.

Designers of children's products have the opportunity to deliver on that promise—sometimes we succeed.

We have progressed (sometimes regressed) through the ages because of our ability to pass our experiences along from one generation to another. Our very survival as a species is related to our ability to avoid danger and stay out of harms way.

Teaching the young to remain safe is vital to survival. But, alas, humans are not the only species to teach their offspring how to survive. What truly separates us from other species is our success in going beyond mere survival. We have profited from our experiences and built on them.

Good design to me is an amalgam of the past, present and future—we learned to make fire, domesticate animals and farm the land. Eventually, we bartered this knowledge with each other and added to our experience by sharing knowledge.

In a sense, this book is about our ability to learn from the past. What really interests me about design is not so much what we create, by why we create.

Good design is more than moving products from factory to showroom to checkout counter. A real need should be filled by the product. How well a design meets the need will affect its ultimate value.

Designing for children requires a very special focus. When selecting products to include in this book, one criteria had priority over all others—*relevancy.* It was essential that the inclusions be designed specifically for children, not just be scaled down versions of adult products.

Following *relevancy,* the other criteria used to measure the success of the products were:

- *Ergonomics*—the design of a product should be easy to use by its intended audience. In the case of children's products they should be scaled to small hands, fingers, feet, toes and so on! For children, this often means just the opposite of small parts; sometimes oversized elements are more appropriate!

  Note: I chose birth to 5 years as the age range for the product targets, because these are the formative years. By age 6, most children are so far developed physically and mentally, that they are capable of performing many adult-oriented activities.

- *Esthetics*—more than just "pretty" colors or shapes, children's products should be inviting and attractive.

  Although infants do not yet possess the sophistication to distinguish subtle variations of colors (nor can many adults), I believe there are far more colors available to the designer than just the primary and secondary pallets.

- *Materials*—an excellent design can sometimes be weakened by the choice of materials in which it is manufactured.

  Too often I have seen wonderful concepts become mediocre because the manufacturer wanted to keep the cost down. True, lower cost means more accessibility to a wider audience; but what is gained in volume is lost in quality.

  Selecting materials is based on numerous factors; cost is only one of them.

- *Durability*—A product should resist breakage (as much for pass-along use as safety).

- *Ease of Manufacture*—Using the correct material lessens down time in production and ultimately keeps cost in line. *Ergonomics* and *esthetics* are often affected by materials.

- *Relevancy*—mentioned earlier, it is a key concern of mine. Having worked within the toy industry for over 15 years, I saw countless products manufactured and sold with little regard for their intrinsic value.

"Wind-up Toys" are examples of products we can probably do without. As entertainment they have limited appeal to all but the youngest child. They are not interactive and beyond teaching a child to turn the wrist clockwise have little redeeming value. I am not saying all products for children must be educational. We all need to be entertained now and then.

Yet, the toy industry has the opportunity more than any other to mold, shape and assist in the development of tomorrow's adults. Fantasy can be healthy, but how many robots, sci-fi war toys and dolls that create tomorrow's "buy me, give me, get me," consumerism do we need?

We do not live in a perfect society. The products in this book have been selected because in some way they illustrate progress and innovation, or have perpetuated tradition by maintaining touch with our past while contributing to our future.

—Stewart Mosberg, FPDC

Chapter 1
Product Manufacturing Guidelines, Government Standards and Regulations

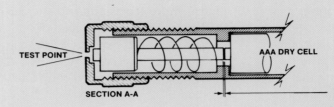

TEST POINT

AAA DRY CELL

SECTION A-A

GAP IS CLOSED UPON INSERTION OF SUFFICIENTLY SHARP POINT TO PASS THRU GAGING SLOT & DEPRESS SENSING HEAD .005. ELECTRICAL CIRCUIT IS THEREBY COMPLETED & INDICATOR TEST LAMP LIGHTS—SHARP POINT FAILS TEST.

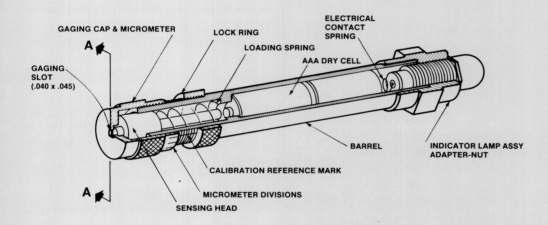

GAGING CAP & MICROMETER

A

GAGING SLOT (.040 x .045)

LOCK RING

LOADING SPRING

ELECTRICAL CONTACT SPRING

AAA DRY CELL

BARREL

INDICATOR LAMP ASSY ADAPTER-NUT

CALIBRATION REFERENCE MARK

MICROMETER DIVISIONS

A

SENSING HEAD

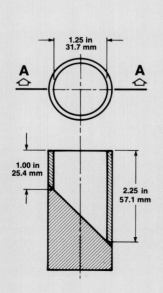

1.25 in
31.7 mm

A   A

1.00 in
25.4 mm

2.25 in
57.1 mm

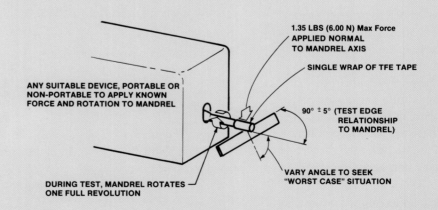

ANY SUITABLE DEVICE, PORTABLE OR NON-PORTABLE TO APPLY KNOWN FORCE AND ROTATION TO MANDREL

1.35 LBS (6.00 N) Max Force APPLIED NORMAL TO MANDREL AXIS

SINGLE WRAP OF TFE TAPE

90° ± 5° (TEST EDGE RELATIONSHIP TO MANDREL)

VARY ANGLE TO SEEK "WORST CASE" SITUATION

DURING TEST, MANDREL ROTATES ONE FULL REVOLUTION

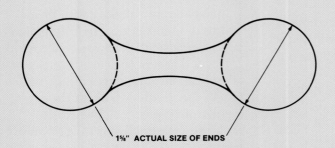

1⅝" ACTUAL SIZE OF ENDS

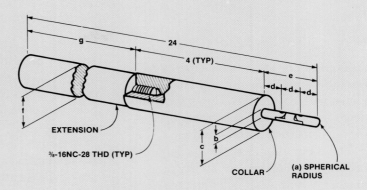

g

24

4 (TYP)

e

d d d

b

c

EXTENSION

⅜-16NC-28 THD (TYP)

COLLAR

(a) SPHERICAL RADIUS

		a	b	c	d	e	f	g
(CHILDREN 0-36 MONTHS INCL.)	PROBE A	.110	.220	1.020	.577	1.731	1	18 9/32
(CHILDREN 37-96 MONTHS INCL.)	PROBE B	.170	.340	1.510	.760	2.280	11/2	17 25/32

ALL DIMENSIONS IN INCHES

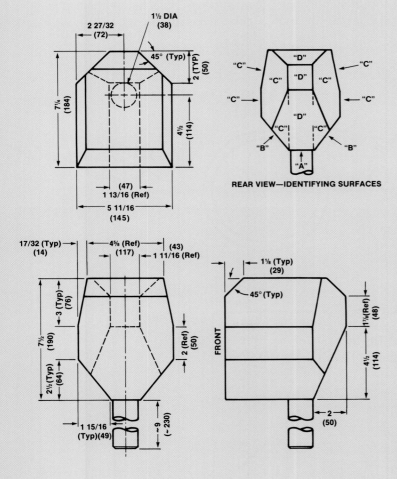

2 27/32
(72)

1½ DIA
(38)

45° (Typ)

2 (TYP)
(50)

7¼
(184)

4½
(114)

(47)

1 13/16 (Ref)

5 11/16
(145)

"C"   "D"   "C"

"C"   "C" "D" "C"

"C"   "D"   "C"

"C"   "C"

"B"   "B"

"A"

REAR VIEW—IDENTIFYING SURFACES

17/32 (Typ)
(14)

4⅝ (Ref)
(117)

(43)

1 11/16 (Ref)

3 (Typ)
(76)

7½
(190)

2 (Ref)
(50)

2½ (Typ)
(64)

1 15/16
(Typ)(49)

9
(~ 230)

1⅛ (Typ)
(29)

45° (Typ)

FRONT

1 7/8 (Ref)
(48)

4½
(114)

2
(50)

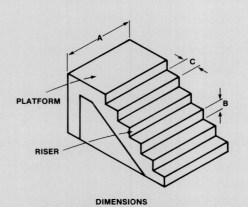

A

C

B

PLATFORM

RISER

DIMENSIONS

"A" SHALL NOT BE LESS THAN 3 FT. (0.92 mm)

"B" SHALL NOT BE LESS THAN 7 IN. (180 mm)

"C" SHALL NOT BE MORE THAN 9 IN. (230 mm)

Is It Safe?

Designing and Buying for Children

As consumers we are at the mercy of the thousands of manufacturers who ply us with toys and clothing, food and drugs, furniture and accessories...all ultimately aimed at our children.

The sheer abundance of available products diminishes our ability to keep pace with what is flammable or shatter-proof, toxic or non-toxic, stable or durable, resilient or destructive.

We rely on a salesperson or the accompanying literature to inform us about the unique features, benefits, precautions, age range or anticipated results of the item's use.

Whether you are a designer of children's products or a concerned parent, it is of some comfort to know guidelines do exist on what is generally recognized as safe and what is potentially harmful.

These rules, regulations and standards help to ensure the child's safety and when a product is in compliance, many labels or products will state as such.

Understanding these guidelines enables the designer to create a more successful product and gives the consumer a chance to make intelligent, responsible purchasing decisions.

Regulations

In the United States, the Department of Commerce's Bureau of Standards is responsible for establishing product standards. Whether pegboards, overalls, car seats or playpens, there are definitive requirements a product must meet before it can be considered safe.

To determine, if in fact, the requirements have been met, there must be testing methods to measure their effectiveness.

The American Society for Testing and Materials (ASTM) is the standard system used by the Consumer Product Safety Commission, an independent agency established by the Consumer Product Safety Act, to protect against unreasonable risks of injury associated with consumer products.

Methodology

The tests, formulas and criteria used are often ingenious and frequently complex. As a matter of interest, we have selected a few of the rules and their respective tests to illustrate the process.

Obviously, those chosen are only cursory examples, but they will give an idea of the scrutiny most products are subjected to.

More detailed and comprehensive information is available from the United States Consumer Product Safety Commission, Washington, DC 20207.

Expectations

It is important to comprehend what a child's capabilities are, physically and mentally. Behavioral norms for a particular age group along with physical proportions will further guide us in the design and purchase choice.

Small Parts

Infants tend to explore with their mouths and it is critical to keep this in mind where small parts are concerned.

Pieces that separate (intentionally or otherwise) must be large enough not to lodge in the throat, block the air passage or be ingested. The ASTM device to measure this is called a *small parts cylinder* and it is designed so a part can be placed at any angle over the opening to simulate possible ingestion. Any object that fits into the opening and falls below the top is considered unsafe.

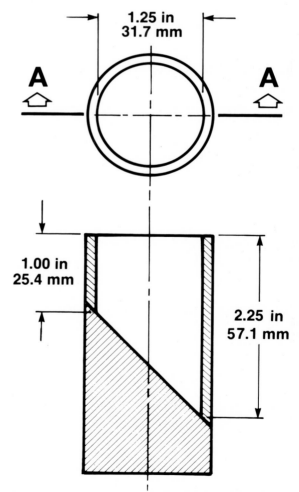

FIGURE A   SMALL PARTS CYLINDER

Rattles

The very prevalent baby rattle should be carefully evaluated for size. Invariably they wind up in an infant's mouth. Beside the obvious concern over ribbons, bells and the noise makers themselves, the entire rattle size must be considered.

The flexibility of a small child's throat is extreme and can hold much larger shapes than you might expect.

The illustration below is of an actual rattle that was lodged in a 6 month old infant's throat after a fall. The above information was made available through a United States Consumer Product Safety Commission fact sheet.

Points, Edges and Corners

Some of the more obvious potential hazards are sharp corners, edges and points. It is best for *all* furniture, toys, accessories, and other children's items to have rounded (preferably large radii) corners, rather than right angles or straight edges. In fact, it's probably a good idea to apply this to adult products as well.

Closely allied to corners are edges. Whether metal, plastic or other material, edges should be curled, rolled or finished to avoid a cutting edge.

An ingenious ASTM device to test for sharp edges is illustrated below.

Sharp points are best avoided, yet sometimes required.

Access to internal mechanisms must be considered and it is imperative that abuse of a product (intended or otherwise) does not reveal hazardous surfaces.

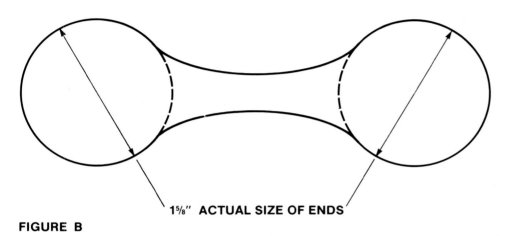

1⅝" **ACTUAL SIZE OF ENDS**

FIGURE B

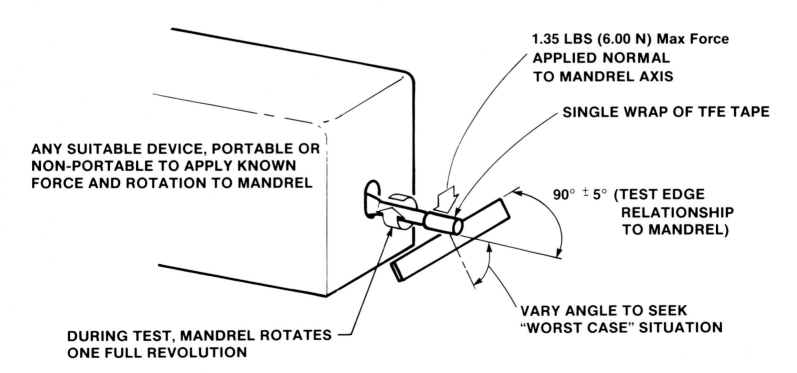

1.35 LBS (6.00 N) Max Force
**APPLIED NORMAL
TO MANDREL AXIS**

SINGLE WRAP OF TFE TAPE

90° ± 5° **(TEST EDGE
RELATIONSHIP
TO MANDREL)**

**ANY SUITABLE DEVICE, PORTABLE OR
NON-PORTABLE TO APPLY KNOWN
FORCE AND ROTATION TO MANDREL**

**VARY ANGLE TO SEEK
"WORST CASE" SITUATION**

**DURING TEST, MANDREL ROTATES
ONE FULL REVOLUTION**

FIGURE C   PRINCIPLE OF SHARP EDGE TEST

Precautions need to be taken to prevent impact or aperture access to small, sharp or electrically charged mechanisms.

Another fascinating test procedure is the sharp point tester. In simple terms, if a point penetrates the opening (located at A-A in the diagram), it will make contact and subsequently light the bulb at the opposite end.

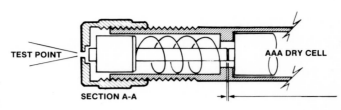

TEST POINT

AAA DRY CELL

SECTION A-A

GAP IS CLOSED UPON INSERTION OF SUFFICIENTLY SHARP POINT TO PASS THRU GAGING SLOT & DEPRESS SENSING HEAD .005. ELECTRICAL CIRCUIT IS THEREBY COMPLETED & INDICATOR TEST LAMP LIGHTS—SHARP POINT FAILS TEST.

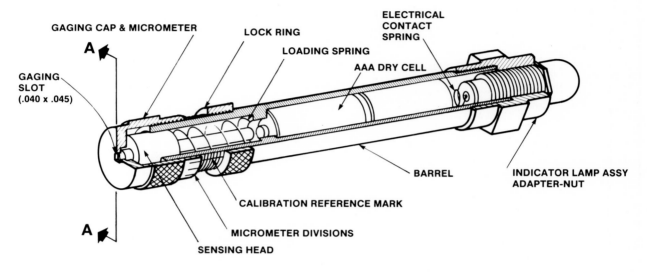

GAGING CAP & MICROMETER

LOCK RING

ELECTRICAL CONTACT SPRING

LOADING SPRING

AAA DRY CELL

GAGING SLOT (.040 x .045)

A

BARREL

INDICATOR LAMP ASSY ADAPTER-NUT

CALIBRATION REFERENCE MARK

A

MICROMETER DIVISIONS

SENSING HEAD

FIGURE D   SHARP POINT TESTER

Accessibility

In the case of accessibility, age plays a role as elsewhere in what is considered safe. The diagram below illustrates an accessibility probe and is predicated on two age groups: (A)0-36 months and (B)37 to 96 months.

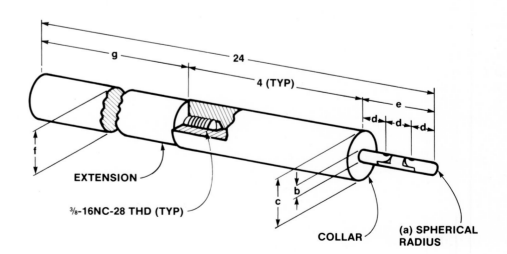

g

24

4 (TYP)

e

d   d   d

f

EXTENSION

c

b

3/8-16NC-28 THD (TYP)

COLLAR

(a) SPHERICAL RADIUS

		a	b	c	d	e	f	g
(CHILDREN 0-36 MONTHS INCL.)	PROBE A	.110	.220	1.020	.577	1.731	1	18 9/32
(CHILDREN 37-96 MONTHS INCL.)	PROBE B	.170	.340	1.510	.760	2.280	11/2	17 25/32

ALL DIMENSIONS IN INCHES

FIGURE E   ACCESSIBILITY PROBES

Steps and Stairs

Steps and stairs are an area that can be easily overlooked. Considering a child's size, open spaces in landings or on risers can allow a child to slip through or get caught. Handrails should be about 8 inches below those of an adult. Steps for children require minimum and maximum dimensional ranges to be considered safe. As a guide, the following diagram indicates the acceptable range.

Cribs

The size of cribs, their decorative and functional components, as well as the accessories meant for inclusion in cribs, such as mattresses, bumpers, and covers are of great concern.

Specific guidelines for full and non-full size cribs are meticulously spelled out by the CPSC. So much of an infant's time is spent in a crib it is appropriate that we include a major portion of the CPSC Requirements in this section:

§ 1508.3 Dimensions.

Full-size baby cribs shall have dimensions as follows:

(a) *Interior.* The interior dimensions shall be 71 ± 1.6 centimeters (28 ± ⅝ inches) wide as measured between the innermost surfaces of the crib sides and 133 ± 1.6 centimeters (52⅜ ± ⅝ inches) long as measured between the innermost surfaces of the crib end panels, slats, rods, or spindles. Both measurements are to be made at the level of the mattress support spring in each of its adjustable positions and no more than 5 centimeters (2 inches) from the crib corner posts or from the first spindle to the corresponding point of the first spindle at the other end of the crib. If a crib has contoured or decorative spindles, in either or both of the sides or ends, the measurement shall be determined from the largest diameter of the first turned spindle within a range of 10 centimeters (4 inches) above the mattress support spring in each of its adjustable positions, to a corresponding point on the first spindle or innermost surface of the opposite side of the crib.

FIGURE F

ILLUSTRATION OF STEP CONSTRUCTION

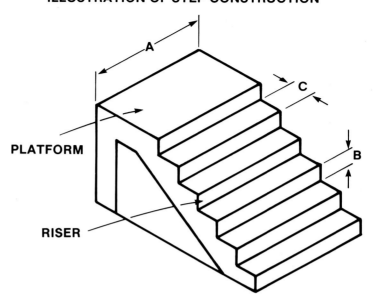

DIMENSIONS

"A" SHALL NOT BE LESS THAN 3 FT. (0.92 mm)

"B" SHALL NOT BE LESS THAN 7 IN. (180 mm)

"C" SHALL NOT BE MORE THAN 9 IN. (230 mm)

(b) *Rail height.* The rail height dimensions shall be as follows:

(1) The height of the rail and end panel as measured from the top of the rail or panel in its lowest position to the top of the mattress support in its highest position shall be at least 22.8 centimeters (9 inches).

(2) The height of the rail and end panel as measured from the top of the rail or panel in its highest position to the top of the mattress support in its lowest position shall be at least 66 centimeters (26 inches).

[38 FR 32129, Nov. 21, 1973; 38 FR 33593 Dec. 6, 1973]

§ 1508.4

Spacing of crib components.

(a) The distance between components (such as slats, spindles, crib rods, and corner posts) shall not be greater than 6 centimeters (2⅜ inches) at any point. Measurement of distance between contoured or irregular slats or spindles shall be done by a 6-centimeter wide by 10-centimeter high by 10-centimeter long (2⅜-

inch wide by 4-inch high by 4-inch long) rectangular block which shall not pass through the space.

(b) The distance between such components shall not exceed 6.3 centimeters (2½ inches) when a 9-kilogram (20-pound) direct force is applied in accordance with the test method in 1508.5. For contoured or irregular slats or spindles, the spacing shall not permit passage of a 6.3-centimeter wide by 8.2-centimeter high by 8.2-centimeter long (2½-inch wide by 3¼-inch high by 3¼-inch long) rectangular block above and below the loading edge when a 9-kilogram (20-pound) direct force is applied in accordance with said test method.

§ 1508.5 Component spacing test method for § 1508.4(b).

(a) Construct a right triangular prism-shaped wedge from a rigid material (steel, wood, aluminum, or equivalent) as shown in diagram.

(b) Place the wedge midway between two vertical components and midway between the top and bottom horizontal rails. Attach a dial push-pull gauge (Chatillon

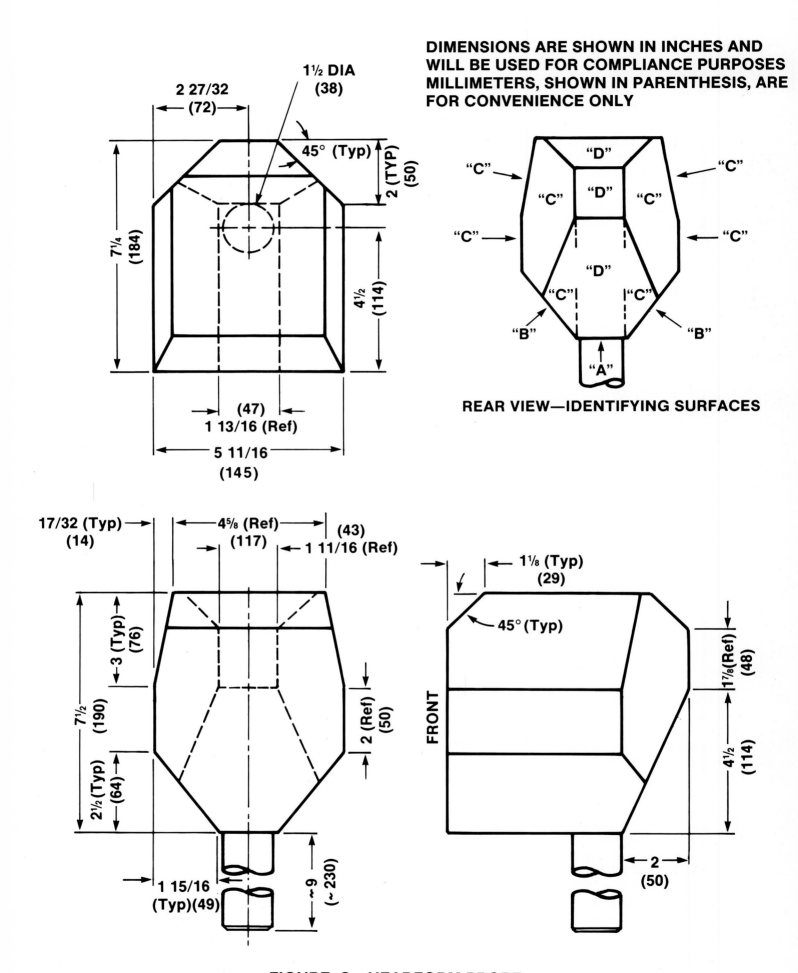

DIMENSIONS ARE SHOWN IN INCHES AND WILL BE USED FOR COMPLIANCE PURPOSES MILLIMETERS, SHOWN IN PARENTHESIS, ARE FOR CONVENIENCE ONLY

REAR VIEW—IDENTIFYING SURFACES

FIGURE G   HEADFORM PROBE

model DPP-50, or equivalent spring scale) to the eyebolt and exert a 9-kilogram (20-pound) direct pull on the wedge. The test may be performed by suspending a 9-kilogram (20-pound) weight from the eyebolt with the crib component placed in a horizontal position.

§ 1508.6 Hardware

(a) A crib shall be designed and constructed in a manner that eliminates from any hardware accessible to a child within the crib the possibility of the hardware's presenting a mechanical hazard through pinching, bruising, lacerating, crushing, breaking, amputating, or otherwise injuring portions of the human body when the crib is in normal use or when subjected to reasonably foreseeable damage or abuse.(b) Locking or latching devices used to secure dropside rails shall require a minimum force of 4.5 kilograms (10 pounds) to activate the release mechanism or shall consist of a double-action device requiring two distinct actions to release.

(c) Wood screws shall not be used in the assembly of stationary sides, dropside rails, folding rails, or stabilizing bars to crib ends or other components that must be removed by the consumer in the normal disassembly of a crib.

§ 1508.7 Construction and finishing.

(a) All wood surfaces shall be smooth and free from splinters. (b) All wood parts shall be free from splits, cracks, or other defects which might lead to structural failure.

(c) Crib end panels and sides or any attachment thereto shall have no horizontal bar, ledge, projection, or other surface accessible to a child inside the crib capable of being used as a toehold located less than 51 centimeters (20 inches) above the mattress support in its lowest position when the side rail is in its highest position, except the lower horizontal bar of the crib rail may have a vertical dimension that extends no higher than 7.6 centimeters (3 inches) above the mattress support in its lowest position. In no case will any gap

between the top surface of the mattress support and the bottom of the lower horizontal rail be permitted. For the purposes of this paragraph, any ledge or projection with a depth dimension greater than 1 centimeter (3/8 inch) shall constitute a toehold.

Cord, Rope and String

Seemingly harmless playpen toys and crib toys may include a length of string that contains hidden dangers. To avoid entanglement cord lengths should not exceed 12 inches.

Hinged Accessories

Folding mechanisms for furniture, toy chests, cabinets and similar items must use hinges that are generally recognized as safe (GRAS) and possess a stop mechanism or locking device.

Flammability

One of the ubiquitous fears for children, as well as adults, is fire. The description of an "extremely flammable solid" substance, as defined by the CPSC, is one that ignites and burns at an ambient temperature of 80° F or less, when subjected to friction, percussion, or electrical spark.

A "Flammable Solid" is one that when tested (see below) ignites and burns with a self-sustained flame at a rate greater than 1/10 of an inch per second along its major axis.

PROCEDURE

Place the prepared sample in a draft-free area that can be ventilated and cleared after each test. The temperature of the sample at the time of testing shall be between 68° F. and 86° F. Hold a burning paraffin candle whose diameter is at least 1 inch, so that the flame is in contact with the surface of the sample at the end of the major axis for 5 seconds or until the sample ignites, whichever is less. Remove the candle. By means of a stopwatch, determine the time of combustion with self-sustained flame. Do not exceed 60 seconds. Extinguish flame with aCO_2 or similar nondestructive type extinguisher. Measure the dimensions of the burnt area and calculate the rate of burning along the major axis of the sample.

ASTM Flammable Solid Test

The ASTM has methods to test potential product abuse and measure durability. There are tests for flexure, torque, compression tension and impact. Procedures exist to verify stability, washability, "tip over" and accidental entrapment.

It should be obvious that many attempts at protecting our safety and the safety of our offspring are being made. Yet, we must still exercise caution and control. It is a general rule of thumb to use common sense when evaluating a purchase. It is the so-called "hidden" dangers that concern us most.

How a product functions or what its intended use really is, must be considered. When it comes to children's products we should remember a very important objective—FUN! It is so much of what being a child is about.

Testing for fun is as simple as watching children use the product. If it is intended to be fun and entertaining then it must be just that. This brings up the issue of age grading. Theoretically, age declarations on a product's package is as much a safety measure as it is an indication of the motor skills or intelligence level required.

Parents and grandparents often over-estimate their child's ability. But just as frequently, they under-estimate them. The latter of these two probably does the greatest injustice to the child since it can postpone joy and learning.

The best method for selecting the product is to know the child. Toys and educational material, for example, should be stimulating, not so difficult as to frustrate, and not so simple as to diminish challenge. By the same token it is wise to consider a child's playmates and siblings. A younger child may gain access to a product intended for an older individual, thereby creating a potential hazard. Caution and forethought are required in such cases.

Understanding degrees of development and progressive stages in a child's growth add significantly to a product's design success. Surely, children vary in their progress. One may be superior in a particular area and slow in another. One child may grow more rapidly than another and ultimately possess a large body while the other remains slight of build with small proportions.

When designing products for all human beings, whether pediatric or geriatric, endomorphic or ectomorphic, it is beneficial to know the variances. These human factors are often referred to as ergonomics and it is a compilation of facts and figures related to size, scale, endurance and strength. It capitalizes on biotechnology, psychology and environmental considerations. Today's product designer has a wealth of knowledge available to work with, and it is their professional responsibility to consider all of it when creating new or improved products.

Size

It is interesting to note the difference in growth rates at varying ages. For example, the length of the body increases 3 1/2 times between birth and adulthood. By 2 years of age, children attain approximately half their adult height. For males this means approximately 34 inches, while body weight increases over 20 times from birth to adulthood. By age 5, the brain has reached 80 percent of adult size and by age 10, almost its complete size has been gained.

The ratio of head to body size is quite fascinating as well: The height of a child's head is significantly larger proportionally to its body as evidenced in this chart:

Average Ratio of Head to Body Height in Children From 0 - 5 Years

Age	Ratio of Head to Body Size
0	4 to 1
3	5 to 1
5	5.5 to 1

The female body length from birth to 4 years of age averages about 1/2 inch less than males and about 1 1/2 pound less. The difference is slight as related to product design in the 0 to 5 year age range.

Great variance occurs when one looks at the upper 5 percent versus the lowest 5 percent of a group, whether measuring height, weight, motor skills or intelligence levels. This is in evidence when studying the following charts:

Height - 5th Percentile Children (Lowest Value)

Age	Height in Inches
1	27
2	29
3	33
4	37
5	40

Weight - 95th Percentile Children (Highest Value)

Age	Weight in Pounds
1	28
2	29
3	42
4	43
5	50

After studying charts and regulations, calculating safety features and potential product abuse the designers' (and consumers') best barometer to gauge a child's product by is to remember what it's like to be a child. The responsibility is great and so are the rewards!

Chapter 2
Toys Recreational

I do not look upon myself as a designer or inventor. Instead, I would call myself a creative interpreter. I absorb many different ideas, processes and materials, then connect them. Then this connection takes place, the first stage of the process of design begins. The more background or exposure one brings to design, the broader the scope and better the focus on the project.

Designing for children is a particularly rewarding and exciting experience. First, it helps to be a parent. It is the quickest way to fully realize the needs of the child as well as understand the concerns of the parent. The product design must truly have a reason for its existence. Is it an improvement or restatement of the same theme? Is there an unfulfilled need to be satisfied?

Safety must be the first consideration in all children's products and must be incorporated into all aspects of design and function. Consideration of materials, angles, toxicity, pinch points and the many unlikely possibilities must be recognized and addressed. I always think of Murphy's Law: "If anything can go wrong, it will go wrong." Designing out problems is a matter of anticipation. Anticipation is a result of many personal experiences with baby products.

Research is an essential part of design. In order to develop a better baby buggy, one must know what came first, second, etc. Why some products were important while others never made it. This includes trip to factories, retail stores, discussions with consumers, focus groups and, of course, actually using those products currently existing in the category of your design/product.

—Michael Newman
President, The Newborne Company

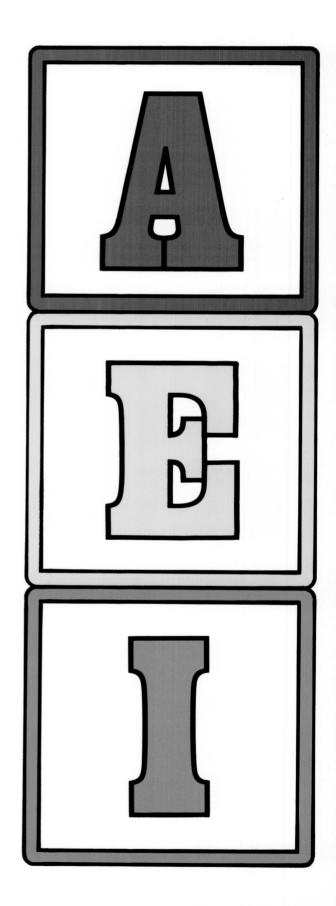

Product: Pool Town
Design Firm: Girsch Design Associates
Design Team: Charles and Maria Girsch and Mark Hammersten; Creative Directors/Tim Moodie; Project Coordinator/Joe Drapcho; Art Director/Mike Damron; Product Designer/ Andrew Plakos; Engineer/ Vicki Evans; Assistant Art Director/Laura Schumacher; Decal Artist and Additional Development, Leisure Design
Client: Mainstreet Toys

A line of pre-school toys designed specifically for play in the backyard pool.

Product: Tubtown
Design Firm: Girsch Design Associates
Design Team: Charles and Maria Girsch
                and Mark Hammersten;
                Creative Directors/Tim
                Moodie; Project
                Coordinator/Joe Drapcho;
                Art Director/Mike
                Damron; Product Designer
                Andrew Plakos; Engineer/
                Vicki Evans; Assistant Art
                Director/Laura
                Schumacher; Decal Artist
                and Additional
                Development, Leisure
                Design
Client: Mainstreet Toys

Tub Town Line is a line of toys for the tub
designed to create a true "town" feel when
they are played with together.

Product: Tubtown
Design Firm: Girsch Design Associates
Design Team: Charles and Maria Girsch
               and Mark Hammersten;
               Creative Directors/Tim
               Moodie; Project
               Coordinator/Joe Drapcho;
               Art Director/Mike
               Damron; Product Designer/
               Andrew Plakos; Engineer/
               Vicki Evans; Assistant Art
               Director/Laura
               Schumacher; Decal Artist
               and Additional
               Development, Leisure
               Design
Client: Mainstreet Toys

A base for the fire boat to come home to with a friendly dalmatian and his dog house, a diving platform, alarm and rainbow handle.

A collection of puzzles that can be taken apart and put back together on the wall of the tub. The material (similar to place mat material) sticks to the wall of the tub and floats too.

Product:	Music Town
Design Firm:	Girsch Design Associates
Design Team:	Charles and Maria Girsch and Mark Hammersten; Creative Directors/Tim Moodie; Project Coordinator/Joe Drapcho; Art Director/Mike Damron; Product Designer/ Andrew Plakos; Engineer/ Vicki Evans; Assistant Art Director/Laura Schumacher; Decal Artist and Additional Development, Leisure Design
Client:	Mainstreet Toys

The central playset of the Musictown line was designed to be a "music sampler" with a variety of instruments. The stage is a drum and tambourine and the microphone has an elastic chord that allows it to be used as a "bass." Above the stage is a bandstand with a xylophone and bells.

Here is the musical vehicle with the rearranged pieces off of the chassis.

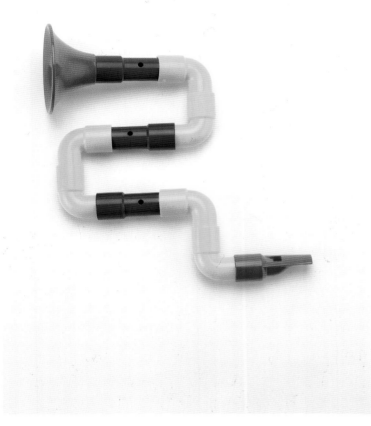

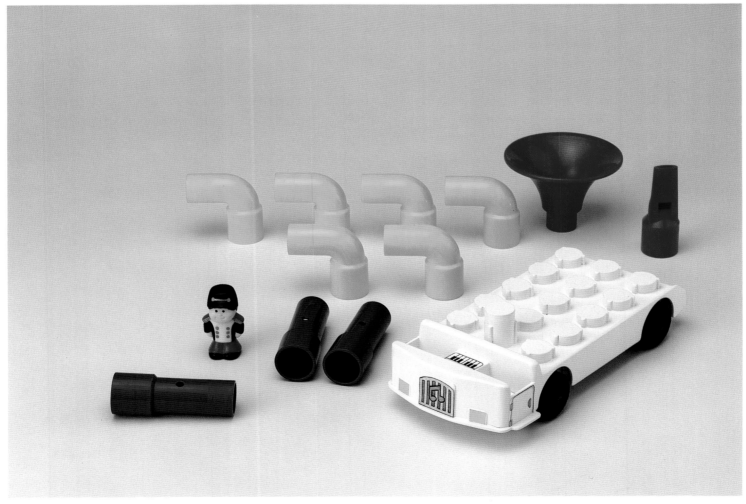

This mini-playset holds a set of six bells in a park-like setting with a slide, swing, stairs and a spot for the band leader to conduct.

This two level bus is actually a double octave, 16 note xylophone. There are spots to store the strikers and a place for the band leader to drive the bus.

A single mold creates the entire base for this mini playset which contains a miniature working keyboard in the sidewalk.

Product: TOP DRAW Re-Markable Top
Designer: Lorna Lippes—Product Development Mgr.
                 David H. Luszcz—Art Director
                 Donald J. Holland Jr.—Asst. Art Director
Client: Brimms Inc.

Children like to draw and Top Draw® allows youngsters to turn their static illustration into a moving, spinning work of art. This toy encourages creativity and gives children a sense of accomplishment regardless of ability. This durable, polystyrene top provides a smooth drawing surface that is stain-resistant. The non-toxic Prong crayons provide good color coverage and are easily erased with a dry paper towel.

Product: Duplo Baby Duck Rattle
Design Firm: The LEGO Group
Client: LEGO Systems, Inc.

The Duplo Baby Line presented a specific design problem: the products had to be safe for infants, while being able to work within the "LEGO system of play." The Baby Duck Rattle meets the challenge by being infant safe and snapping together with other Duplo products. In this way, when the child becomes too old to play with a rattle, it can become part of the LEGO system and used as a piece for more advanced sets.

Product: Duplo Pre School Fire Engine
Design Firm: The LEGO Group
Client: LEGO Systems, Inc.

This five-piece set locks together to form a fire engine complete with a hose, ladder and fireman. The colorful ABS plastic is non-toxic and sturdy enough to last through many hours of hard play.

Product: LEGO Basic Building Set
Design Firm: The LEGO Group
Client: LEGO Systems, Inc.

LEGO has been a childhood favorite for many years; their bright non-toxic colors and interchangeable, interlocking pieces allow a child's imagination free reign. With the addition of LEGO trees, people, working doors and wheels, the possibilities are endless.

Product: Construction Train
Design Firm: Brio Toys AB
Designer: Ingvar Petersson
Client: Brio Scanditoy Corporation

The Brio Construction Train is designed with the imaginative preschooler in mind. Motor skills and color recognition are developed with the use of this durable, yet safe toy. The train has no sharp edges and connects with magnets; bright non-toxic paints are used to color removable wooden blocks in various shapes. This toy is a Parents' Choice Award winner.

Product: Look-A-Saurus Wood Puzzles

Designer: John Daniel Smith

Design Firm: Graphics-Color Associates, Ltd.

Client: Small World Toys

These wooden puzzles show authentically detailed dinosaurs in their natural habitats. When the first layer is removed, the dinosaur's skeleton is revealed. As the puzzle helps the child develop their coordination skills, they also show dinosaur bone structures. Each puzzle has a different number of pieces that fit properly with no small parts or sharp points.

Product: Flexiblock ®
Designer: Ron Lyman
Client: Fantasy Toys, Inc.

FLEXIBLOCKS stack easily top to bottom and snap end-to-end to form a unique pivoting action. These patented features enable FLEXIBLOCKS to move, twist and bend. Motion encourages the creation of wonderful structures--ranging from dinosaurs with arms that move and mouths that open to masks and jewelry that children can actually wear! FLEXIBLOCKS use a simple two block system to accomplish all of this fun, and the larger size of these blocks makes them attractive to Preschool children because they are easy to manipulate. As a child becomes older, more challenging structures can be built using the same blocks.

Flexiblocks are the only product to win the highest award in toy tests conducted by ABC and CBS television news two years in a row! They are a Parents' Choice Foundation Award Winner and are featured in the book THE RIGHT TOYS, by Dr. Helen Boehm. All of these awards are given to toys that are educational, creative, safe—and have superior play value.

Product: Matchbox (Range)
Design Firm: Knut Hartmann Design
Design Team: Knut Hartmann; Art Director, President/Regine Hany; Designer
Client: Matchbox Spielwaren Gmbh

Matchbox has been for years the maker of the most authentic scaled-down versions of real cars, trucks, and motorcycles. Kids will spend hours upon hours playing with the "real thing."

Product: Woodles
Design Firm: Playskool Design Group
Client: Hasbro Incorporated

Woodles combine bright colors with natural wood, which gives Woodles a quality appearance as well as weight for a good rolling car. Plastic adds color, durability, and allows for play features. Each Woodles head is soft making them easy to grab and squeeze.

Product: Little Carrier
Designer: Bjorn Alskog
Client: Playsam Activity Toys, Division of Kalmarsunds-Gruppen, Kalmar, Sweden

This cart provides children with a handy way to transport friends and toys. The epoxy-lacquered steel tubing and waterproof plywood provide sturdy support. Solid rubber tires with ball-bearings in front and nylon-bearings in the rear provide for a smooth ride. All exposed edges are smoothed or curved and the bright colors appeal to the most discriminating toddler.

Product: Woodles
Design Firm: Playskool Design Group
Client: Hasbro Incorporated

Woodles combine bright colors with natural wood, which gives Woodles a quality appearance as well as weight for a good rolling car. Plastic adds color, durability, and allows for play features. Each Woodles head is soft making them easy to grab and squeeze.

Product: My First Buddys
Design Firm: Herstein/Schecterson Incorporated
Client: Buddy L. Corporation

An Australian Toy Association "Toy of the Year Award" winner, My First Buddys are recreational toys which are built to last. The simplicity of form and proper ergonomic shape make these toys easy to handle and play with. Simple action, high quality and low retail prices make these toys fun, strong, economical, and treasured by children.

Product: Little Tikes® Play House
Design Firm: Notthingham-Spirk Design
         Associates
Client: The Little Tikes Company

This playhouse comes complete with working shutters, a dutch door, table and chairs, and a telephone. Made of sturdy polyethylene this house will stand up to the elements and rough play better than a standard wooden playhouse.

Product: Flashlight
Design Firm: Playskool Design Group
Client: Hasbro, Inc.

The Playskool Flashlight features an automatic shut off, if the flashlight is left unattended for 30 seconds, has a durable, plastic body, and beams with red, green or white light for colorful play.

Product:	Sof-Blox™ Foam Blocks
Designer Team:	Bill Walsh, President
	Christopher T. Walsh, Inventor
	Daniel P. Walsh, Packaging
Design Firm:	3 W Designers Inc.

These polyfoam blocks come in five colors, eleven shapes and two sizes; deluxe and jumbo, which are 31 times as big as the deluxe blocks and make for larger than life fun for kids. The variety of shapes and sizes give children more play value—they can use them as building blocks, as part of a variety of games, to create puzzles or spellout letters and words for hours of quiet fun.

The durable foam is safe and non-toxic and meets consumer Product Safety Commission Standards. The blocks are made in the USA and have been awarded patent number .

Product:	Party Kitchen
Designer:	James Mariol
Design Firm:	Design Alliance
Client:	The Little Tikes Company

This play kitchen is better designed and equipped than many apartment kitchens. The table folds down when not in use to make the unit easy to store. The stove has knobs that turn and the oven door opens and there is a rack to hold casseroles. The sink comes complete with a moving faucet and a rack for drying dishes. A coffee machine is built in and there is a phone mounted for convenience.

Product: Turtle Sandbox
Designer: Charlie Tyke
Client: The Little Tikes Company

The shell of this giant green turtle can be removed to reveal a sand box. The durable polyethylene cover not only keeps the sand in place but also keeps the elements out. Kids will delight in this design, especially since the turtle is tough enough for kids to climb on when it is together.

Product: "TUFF STUFF" Vacuum Cleaner/Movie Camera, Drill, Chain Saw/Shopping Basket

Designer: Gerry Leistikow—Designer/Research Project Mgr.

Client: Mattel Toys

These toys allow children to "play act" at adult activities with scaled-down, safe models of their real-life counterparts.

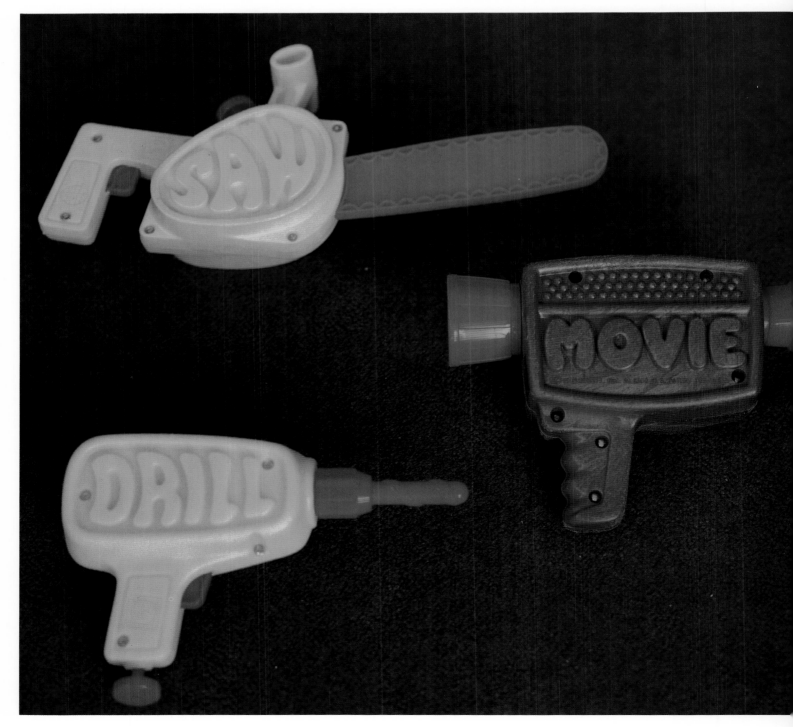

Product: The Minicruiser
Designer: Morton L. Heilig
Design Firm: Supercruiser, Inc.

This two-wheel scooter is designed with safety in mind. Hand brakes allow the rider to stop the scooter.

Product: The Supercruiser Scooter
Designer: Morton L. Heilig
Design Firm: Supercruiser, Inc.

This scooter will provide your child with many hours of fun and exercise.

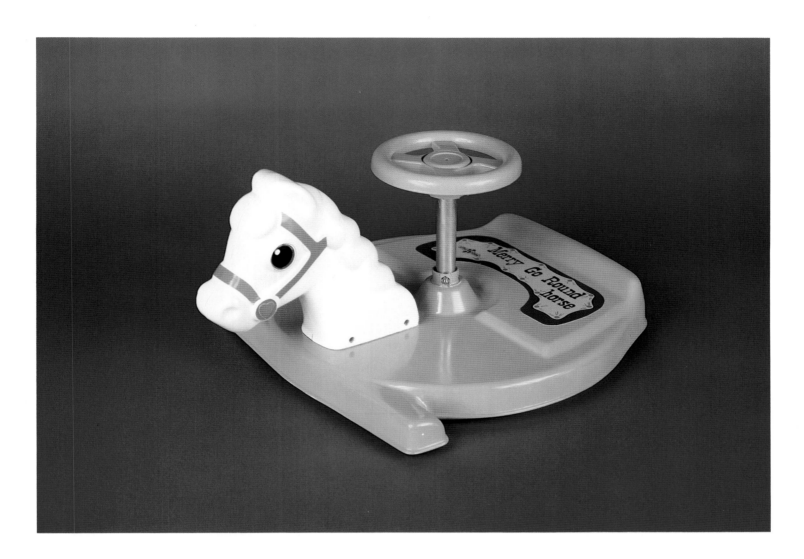

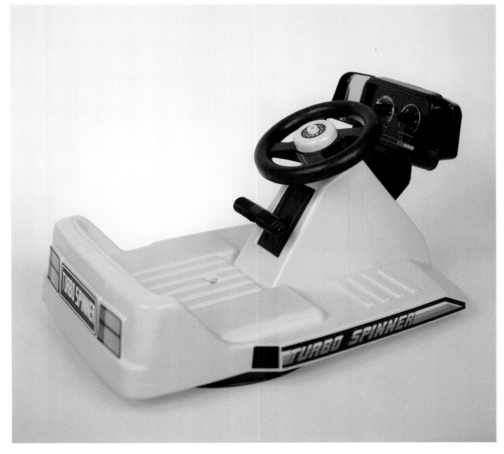

Product: Turbo Spinner/Horse-go-
Round
Designer: Ron Klawitter
Client: Steven Mfg. Co.

Designed to simulate a racing car or a
merry-go-round, these indoor riding toys
can be spun in either direction by a small
child. The product meets all safety and
industry standards for American made
toys. Handicapped children who lack full
use of their legs, enjoy playing with this
toy due to the real sensation of speed as
the Turbo Spinner turns.

Product: Cozy Coupe Car®
Client: The Little Tikes Company

This colorful car, complete with rumble seat, provides many hours of fun for young drivers.

Product: Sport Coupe Racer
Client: The Little Tikes Company

Large wheels and sturdy polyethylene make this sport coupe racer a durable plaything.

Product: Giraffe/Reindeer

Designed to encourage children to keep their playroom tidy, the saddle functions as the toy box lid and the projections off the animal heads are useful for hanging up clothes. This design also allows for the head and neck of the animals to be packed inside the toy body to make shipping cartons smaller.

Product: Toddler Swing
Client: The Little Tikes Company

This sturdy polyethylene swing is supported by four nylon ropes for durability and safety. The blue "handlebar" provides a place for the child to hold on without having to grasp the ropes.

Product: Carousel Rocking Horse
Designer: LaMarr Benton
Client: Woods by Hartco, Inc.

What child can resist a carousel ride, the lively music, the bright colors and the pretty horses? The spirit of all this is captured by these beautifully trimmed solid pine rocking horses. Available in two sizes and a variety of colorful trims, these horses bring the amusement park home for children to enjoy every day.

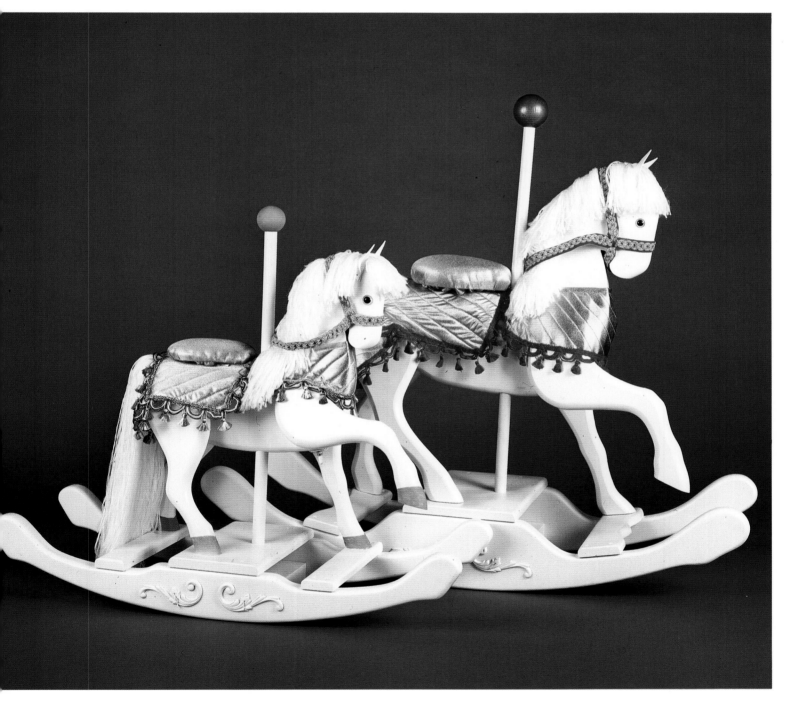

Product: Change-Around Truck
Client: The Little Tikes Company

This brightly colored truck has pivotal
action to provide your child with hours of
fun.

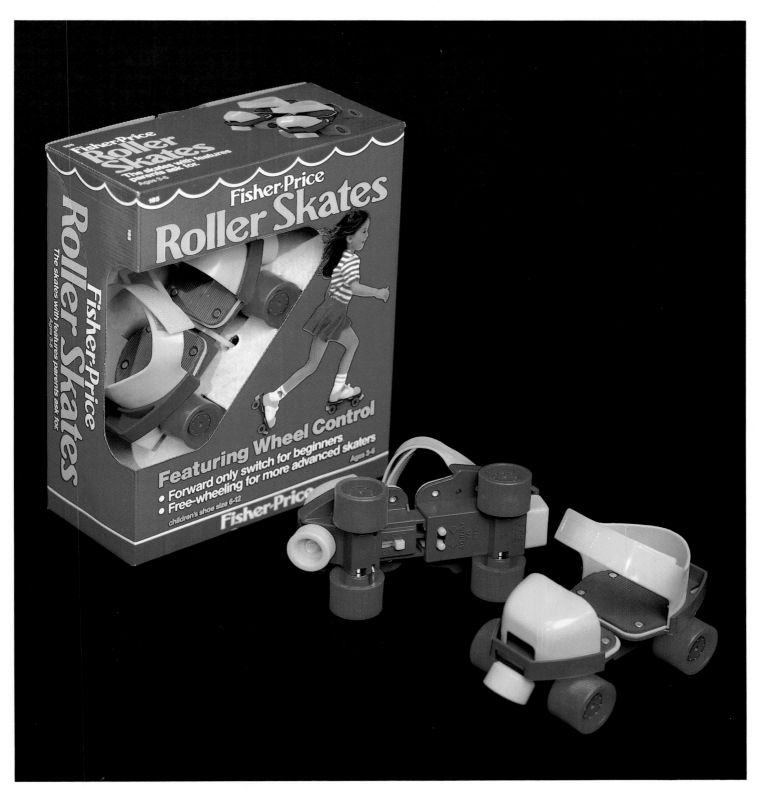

		The unique design of these skates was
Product:	Pre-School Trainer Skates	featured on the cover of Modern Plastics
Designer:	Rueben Klamer: Concept	Magazine in December 1987 as a
	and Development	"Triumph of Design." Designed for pre-
	Robert Mortonson:	schoolers as training skates, they have a
	Industrial Designer	switch that prevents the skate wheel from
	Beatrice Pardo: Industrial	spinning freely so a young child can gain
	Designer	the feeling of stability before switching the
Design Firm:	Rueben Klamer Toy Lab	skate back to free-wheeling, forward and
Client:	Fisher Price	reverse wheels. The flexible vinyl straps

The unique design of these skates was featured on the cover of Modern Plastics Magazine in December 1987 as a "Triumph of Design." Designed for pre-schoolers as training skates, they have a switch that prevents the skate wheel from spinning freely so a young child can gain the feeling of stability before switching the skate back to free-wheeling, forward and reverse wheels. The flexible vinyl straps have velcro closures for ease and fastening adjustability.

Product:	Pop Up Pitcher and Catcher
Design Firm:	Hasbro Incorporated
Design Team:	Preschool Design Group
Client:	Hasbro Incorporated

It's major league excitement just for kids! Little sluggers step on the pedal so the pitcher can toss the ball for them to hit. If they miss, the pitcher will catch the ball so they can try again without having to chase after scattered baseballs. This toy helps build confidence while developing good batting skills.

Product: Tap-A-Tune® Piano
Designer: Walt Doe
Client: The Little Tikes Company

This toy piano is made of polyethylene for strength and steel keys for superior sound quality. The color-coded keys allow even a child who does not read to easily follow the accompanying song book and play their favorite songs.

Chapter 3

Furniture

Baby products should be simple to understand and use. My goal is to design a product that requires no instruction sheet. The product should be self-explanatory. This, of course, is only a direction. We do have need for a clear, precise instruction sheet.

Materials are a crucial element of design. The selection of a new material often will create a totally different effect or image for that product. The material is the aesthetics of the design. The orchestration of these materials combined with the vision of the product line and contour is what makes up style.

Make no mistake about it, style is what sells baby products. A design must look right first, then the customer considers function. Safety should be presumed to be part of the design.

Finally, a product/design must fit neatly into the lifestyle of the parent/parents. Does the product allow for the child to travel or be carried easily, sleep or play comfortably? In short, is the product incorporating the needs of both the child and the parent?

—**Michael Newman**, *President*
The Newborne Company

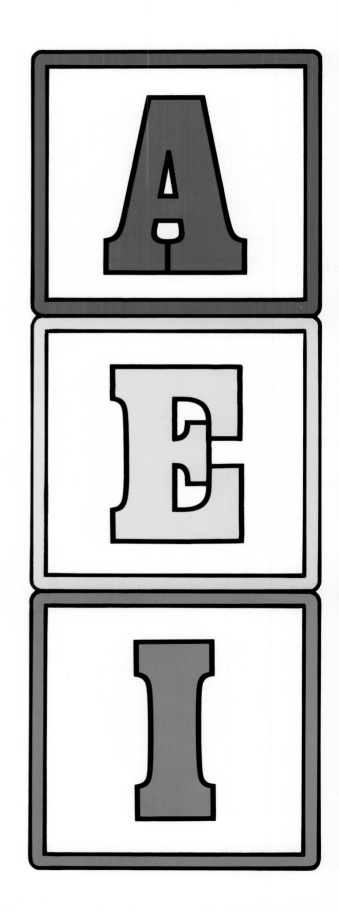

Product: Crib and Trumble
Design Team: Nestor Bromberg
Leon Sztern
Client: Puck Children's Furniture,
Inc.

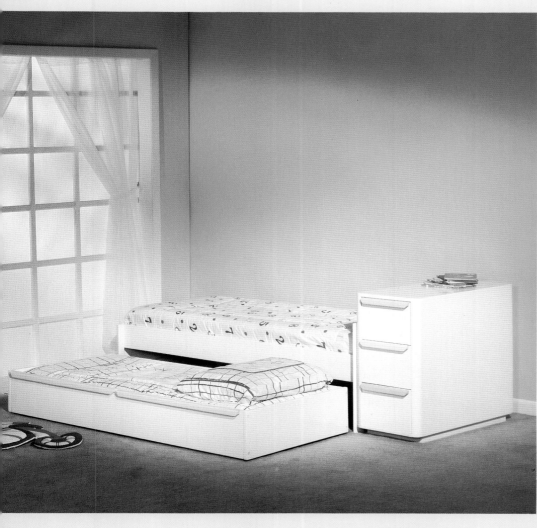

This innovative crib is designed to convert from a crib to a double youth bed. As a crib it features a three drawer chest and a large drawer for storage. The three drawer chest, the crib railing and the lower drawer divider are removable for easy conversion. The lower drawer includes ball casters so it is easy to use as a trundle bed. This makes it perfect for a sleep-over, or weekend guests.

Product:	Whitco Storage Wall Storage
Design Team:	Griffin M. Stabler, President
	Richard Barr, Designer
	Charles Kaplan, Lake Shore Curriculum
Client:	Whitney Bros. Co.

These storage modules offer cleanable and flexible storage systems for the preschool and day care market. They provide attractive, usable space for youngsters and their belongings. The primary colors and maple trim bring visual interest to this institutional furniture.

Product:	First Class
Design Firm:	The Newborne Company
Design Team:	Michael Newman: President/Jim Dodge: Sales Manager
Client:	The Newborne Company

The Newborne Company introduces the First Class Desk, a versatile activity center for young minds. Designed to fit the needs of growing children from ages 3 to 6 years, it's a place to develop drawing and other motor skills. Featuring smooth clean lines and an integrated seat and desk top, the unit is built of sturdy powder coated steel, and features a sliding coated wire drawer large enough to handle a variety of accessories.

Product: Cradle
Design Firm: The Newborne Company
Design Team: Michael Newman: President/Jim Dodge: Sales Manager
Client: The Newborne Company

The Gliding Cradle measures 36″ by 18″. The lightweight yet sturdy cradle comes complete with clown print mattress pad and a "swing-lock" system for safety. The cradle can be used as either a stationary or gliding cradle. Simply by removing one side, the cradle converts into a swinging daybed or a child's swing which may be used indoors or outdoors due to its weather-resistant construction.

Product: Big Table and Chairs
Design Team: Kevin R. Aker, I.D.S.A.,
Design Director
Robert L. Houry, Industrial
Designer
Design Firm: Little Tikes Design
Client: The Little Tikes Company

This table and chair set has a foam-filled top for added strength and safety, with column-like legs for stability. A drawer provides storage for crayons or small toys; the table is designed for easy use with plenty of room for a child to pull their chairs in close in order to work or play.

Product: Picnic Table
Designer: John Sinchok
Client: The Little Tikes Company

This scaled-down picnic table can be used indoor and out. It is proportioned so a small child can comfortably eat or play at the table and is made of durable polyethylene to survive varying weather conditions and rough play.

Product: Safe Keeper II
Design Team: Bonnie Chew and Joan Chew
Client: Lil' Lamb's Keeper Incorporated

The Safe Keeper II, a portable play pen designed with new safety corners responds to baby's movements with comforting motion. The Lil' Lamb's Keeper is designed for safety with quality features that include: no drop sides, no hinges, no exposed interior surfaces, no locking pieces and security corners.

Product: Travel Keeper II
Design Team: Bonnie Chew and Joan Chew
Client: Lil' Lamb's Keeper Incorporated

Lil' Lamb's Travel Keeper Portable Through-The-Door Baby Bed and Travel Pen is useful both at home and on vacation. Available in three lively colors. The Baby Bed and Travel Pen is also machine washable.

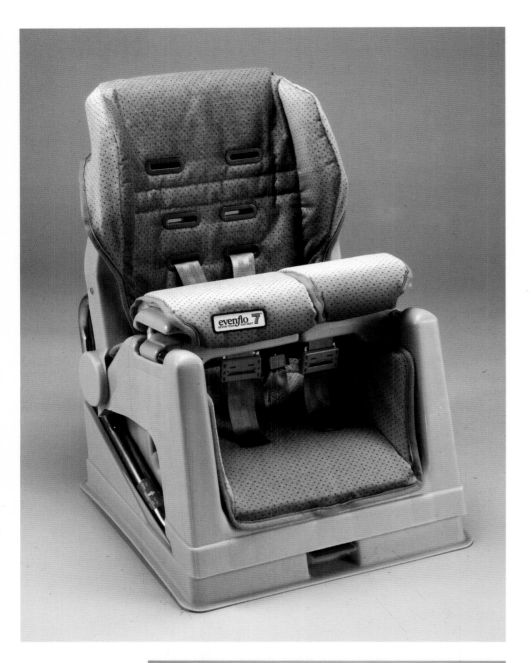

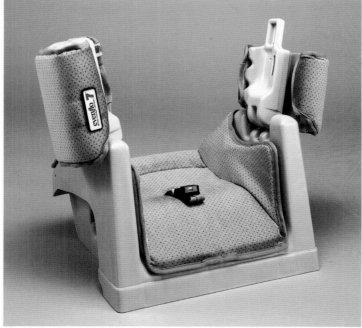

Product: 7 Year Car Seat
Designer: Jim Kain: In House Designer
Client: Evenflo Juvenile Furniture
Company

The Evenflo Car Seat was designed to be strong and durable and to maintain a good fit for all the various weights and sizes of children up to the age of 7. The car seat meets all test standards in all modes of use, and they provide easy conversion between car seat and booster seat.

Product:	Century 570 Infant Car Seat
Design Team:	Robert D. Wise: Manager, Research & Development/ Paul K. Meeker: Product Designer/Mark A. Sedlack; Product Designer
Client:	Century Products/Gerber Furniture Group

The Century 570 Infant Car Seat comes with full frontal safety strap and has passed all U.S. government required crash testing for safety.

Product: Kanga-Rocka-Roo
Designer: Robert D. Wise: Manager, Research and Development
Client: Century Products/Gerber Furniture Group

The Kanga-Rocka-Roo Baby Carrier is a safe and easy way to bring your infant almost anywhere. Constructed of polyethylene, ABS and vinyl, the Kanga-Rocka-Roo is both durable and helpful.

Product: Commander I
Design Team: Robert D. Wise: Manager, Research & Development/ Steve Justice: Product Designer
Client: Century Products/Gerber Furniture Group

The Commander I Car Seat is for children from the ages of 2 to 8. The Commander has passed all U.S. government required car testing for safety. The Commander is lightweight and durable, making it easy to transfer from car to car.

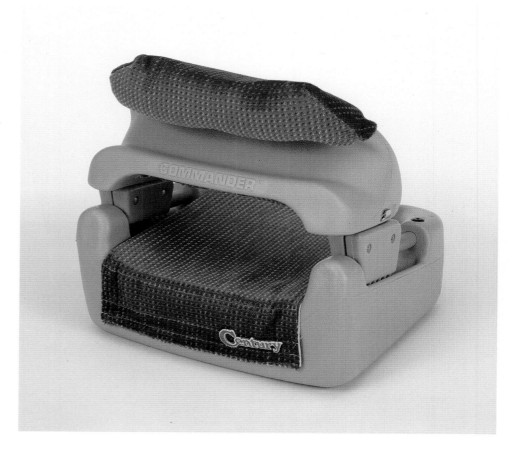

Product: Century 1000,2000,3000,
Ste Series
Design Team: Robert D. Wise: Manager,
Research and Development/
Paul Meeker: Product
Designer/Mark A. Sedlack,
Product Designer
Client: Century Products/Gerber
Furniture Group

The Century Car Seats for infants are
constructed of L.D. polypropylene and
have passed all U.S. government required
crash testing. The car seats were designed
to be strong and durable and to maintain a
good fit for all infants up to 40 pounds.

Product:	Century 580 Infant Car Seat Deluxe
Design Team:	Robert D. Wise: Manager, Research and Development/ Paul Meeker: Product Designer/Mark A. Sedlack, Product Designer
Client:	Century Products/Gerber Furniture Group

The Century Infant Car Seat Deluxe comes with a full frontal strap for added protection and a carry-all bag for easy conversion. Constructed of H.D. polyethylene, the durable Century car seat fits infants from birth to the age of 18 months. The Century Infant Car Seat Deluxe won the National Independent Nursery Furniture Retailers Association Product Of The Year Award for 1987.

Product:	Evenflo Swing
Designer:	Joe Casagrande: In House Designer
Client:	Evenflo Juvenile Furniture Company

The Evenflo Swing provides a natural swinging motion for baby's ease and comfort. The swing seat disconnects easily and can be used as a car seat or a carrier. Getting baby in an out of the Evenflo Swing is done with ease and its versatility will be a real help to parents.

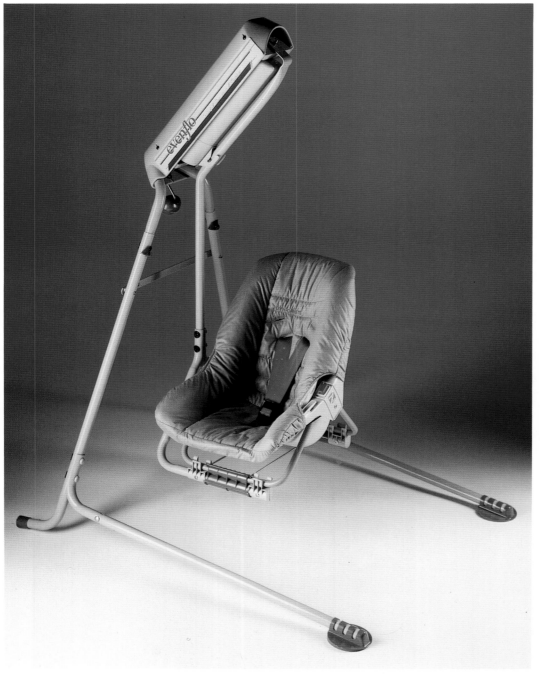

Product: Bassinet
Design Firm: Badger Basket Company
Client: Badger Basket Company

The Badger Basket Company Bassinet is beautifully constructed for baby's comfort. The bassinet's accessories include a metal stand on wheels for easy maneuverability, and securely fastened straps which serve as handles.

Product: Potty Training Chair and Feeding Chair
Design Firm: The Badger Basket Company
Client: The Badger Basket Company

The Badger Basket Company's infant potty training chair and feeding chair are versatile and easy to clean. Constructed of wood, steel and vinyl, these well-designed chairs will make feeding time and toilet training easier.

Product: Natasa Child's Cot
Designer: Biba Bertok, Ljubljana, Yugoslavia
Client: Slovenijales, Ljubljana, Yugoslavia

This durable child's cot allows young sleepers to rest securely, without fear of falling out of bed. Wheels located at one end provide easy maneuverability, and the linen fabric serving as the ends, provides a safe headboard.

Product: High Chair
Design Firm: Nottingham-Spirk Design
Associates
The Little Tikes Company
Design Department
Client: The Little Tikes Company

This high-tech highchair is a far cry from the chairs of our youth. With a wide based support structure, an oversized sliding tray, and a seat with side arms and a foot rest, both mother and child have been considered in the redesign of this childhood standard.

Made of sturdy lightweight polyethylene, the chair allows even the most restless child room to move around, but does not allow him or her to slip out or tip the chair over. For the parent, in addition to the added safety features, the chair has a large tray and is made of easy to clean materials, so a novice eater's mess will be confined to a small, easy to clean area

Product: "Lili" Writing Table and
Blackboard for Children
Designer: Tatjana Coloni, Ljubljana,
Yugoslavia
Client: Slovenijales, Ljubljana,
Yugoslavia

This lacquered chipboard table and chalkboard is durable and attractive. Hinged drawers allow easy access to stored items. Peg and hole construction allows the height of the table to be adjusted according to the youngster's growth and comfort.

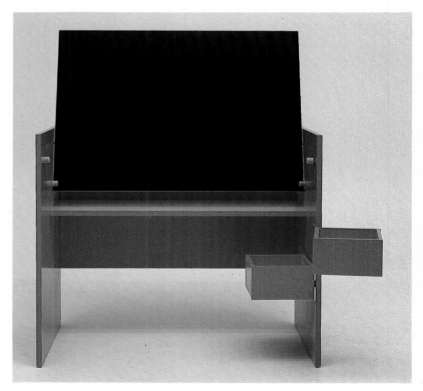

Product: Gerber High Chair
Design Team: Robert D. Wise: Manager, Research and Development/ Robert Quilan: Project Engineer/Ronald S. Carter: Designer
Client: Century Products/Gerber Furniture Group

The Gerber High Chair is constructed of H.D. polypropylene, ABS and metal tubing which is durable and meets all safety standards. The high chair gives ample back support and foot support for infants of various weights and sizes.

Product: Young Generation Crib and Bed

Design Team: Brian Elvidge: President/ Jerry Schwartz: President

Client: Young Generation Furniture, Limited

This is an adjustable crib and bed for today and tomorrow. At the infant stage, a two-position mattress support offers easier accessibility for parents. Later on, the crib and bed converts to a junior bed and matching three drawer unit.

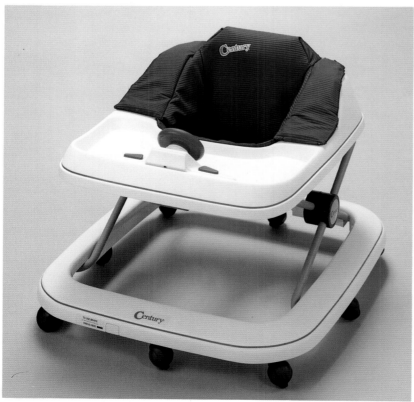

Product: Custom Coupe
Design Team: Robert D. Wise: Manager,
Research and Development/
Paul Meeker: Product
Designer/Mark A. Sedlack:
Product Designer
Client: Century Products/Gerber
Furniture Group

The Custom Coupe Walker allows your child to explore their world on their own, and helps to develop leg coordination and balance to aid in the early stages of walking. The walker has various functions such as a bouncer built within to allow for more body movement and an adjustable braking system for child's safety.

Product:	Seamore The Action Seahorse
Design Firm:	Sid Tepper Incorporated
Design Team:	Robert D. Wise: Manager, Research and Development/ Paul Meeker; Product Designer/Jairo Miller: Product Designer

Seamore The Action Seahorse makes bath-time fun time for children. Suction cups which adhere to the tub keep Seamore in one place. Constructed of H.I. Styrene and polyethylene, Seamore The Action Seahorse is durable and makes bathing easier.

Product:	Child's Rocking Chair
Designer:	Gerry Leistikow
Client:	G. Leistikow "Designs in Wood"

The company objective of the "creation of quality real furniture for young people" is clearly met in this handsome rocking chair. Made of finely finished wood and leather the chair's long, laid back design makes it almost impossible for a youngster to tip over.

Product:	Kiddi Comfort™
Designer:	Margaret A. Alivizatos
Design Firm:	Masinali Designs
Client:	Comfort Products

A wonderfully useful, practical, cozy nap mat or comforter, Kiddi Comfort is as good for a small baby. It is made up of four sections, each with a polystyrene bead-filled pillow inserted through a handy zippered opening, so that it is machine wash and dryable both inside and out. The mat gently molds to the child's body and is thermally insulated to protect the child against drafts.

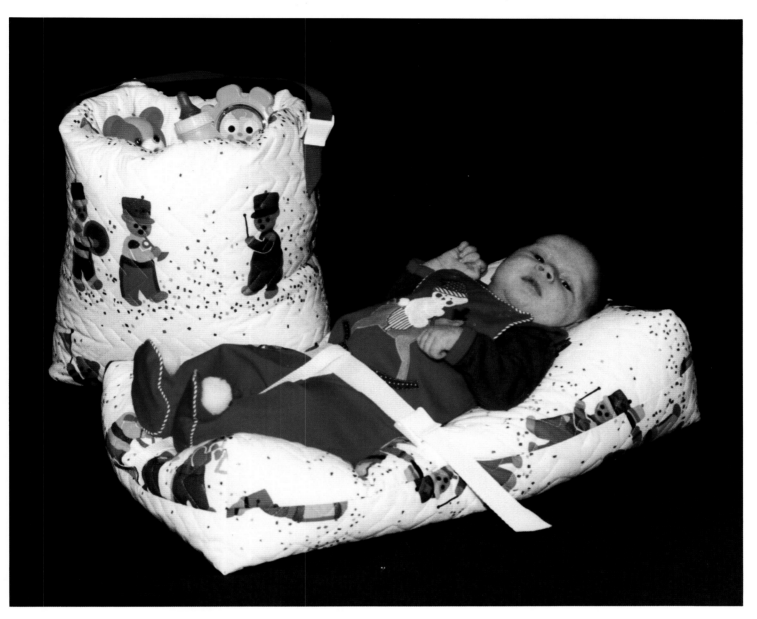

Product:	Comfort Tote™
Designer:	Margaret A. Alivizatos
Design Firm:	Masinali Designs
Client:	Comfort Products

A truly lightweight portable and convertible bed/bag duo comfort tote may be used alone on any surface or in a shipping cart. Designed for infants up to six months old its hospital proven design provides orthopedic support for baby's head, neck and spine. It is machine washable and dryable and its special insulating properties keep baby cool in the summer and warm in the winter.

Product:	Juvenile Rocker
Design Firm:	Foam Merchants Incorporated
Design Team:	Stuart Schrift: President/ Abram Lozano: Plant Manager & Designer
Client:	Foam Merchants Incorporated

The Juvenile Rocker creates a total living environment within the children's living space. The rocker is functional and fun for kids and comes in colors that kids will love. The rocking chair rocks evenly and opens into a sleeper.

Product:	Juvenile Dinosaur Chair
Design Firm:	Foam Merchants Incorporated
Design Team:	Stuart Schrift: President/ Abram Lozano: Plant Manager & Designer
Client:	Foam Merchants Incorporated

What child doesn't love a dinosaur? This durable, safe and lightweight chair will be loved by children for their looks and comfort. The Dinosaur Chair opens up easily to a sleeper, making them great for little overnight guests.

Product: Playcraft® Storage Chest
Designer: Robert Houry
Designer Firm: In-House
Client: The Little Tikes Company

This sturdy chest has plenty of room for toys, games, and stuffed animals. The top is removable and light enough for a small child to life off and there is no danger of a child's hand getting caught in the lid. When the storage chest is closed, it is sturdy enough for a child to use as a bench.

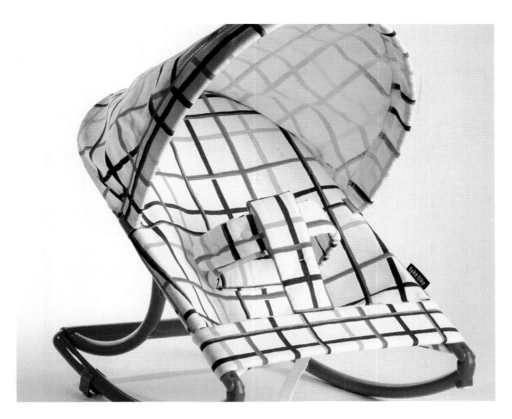

Product: Tyke Hike Baby Rocker
Designer: Mike Wilson: In House Designer
Client: Tyke Corporation

To keep a baby content, no matter where you are, is the number one problem with infants. The natural rocking motion of the Tyke-hike Baby Rocker quickly calms baby down, or puts baby to sleep. A baby is comfortable in the extra-deep seat, and is held snugly and safely by the extra wide, padded tummy belt.

Product: Tyke Hike Chair
Designer: Mike Wilson: In House Designer
Client: Tyke Corporation

Whether it's playing house or playing rough, the Tyke-hike Chair is made for it. At a picnic, on the beach, or even in a wading pool (it's 100 percent waterproof), the Tyke-hike Chair will accompany even the youngest child. Its frame is smooth, fully rounded and lightweight (under 2 pounds). The Tyke-hike Chair will stand up to a lot of sitting, and whatever else your child has in mind.

Product: Joy Ride Convertible Infant Car Seat/Carrier

Designer: Paul Meeker: Contract Designer

Client: Evenflo Juvenile Furniture Company

The Joy-Ride Convertible Car Seat with Carrier has a canopy to protect your child from the sun. The car seat is constructed of polypropylene for strength and toughness, and comes with a tray in front to hold baby's belongings, and also a storage compartment in back.

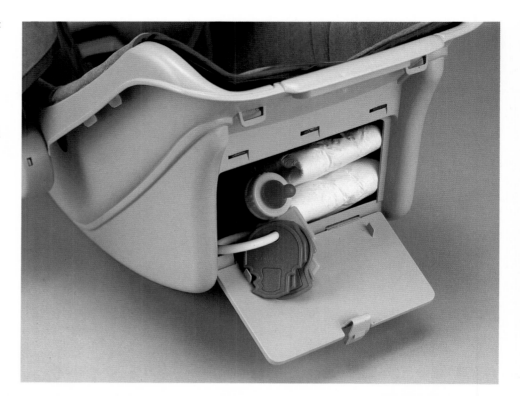

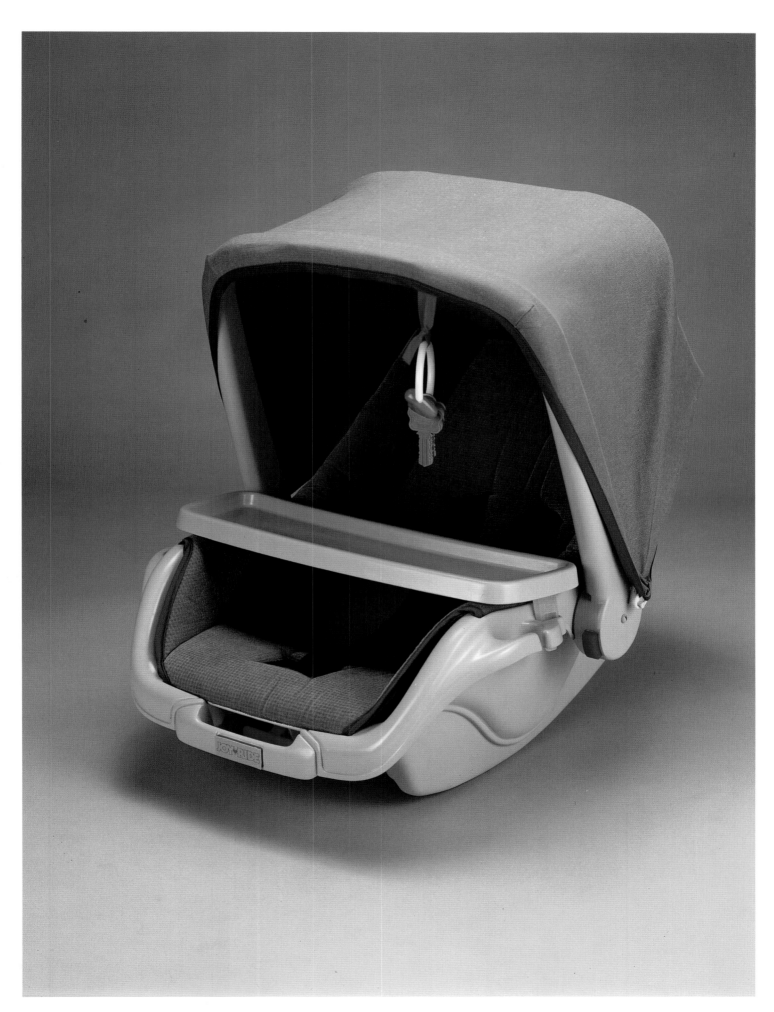

Product:	Maclaren X76 Royalty Stroller
Design Firm:	Andrews Maclaren Limited
Design Team:	(Marshall) Ken Kaiser: Vice President, Juvenile Division; (Maclaren) Ken Senior: Export Sales Manager/Peter Hawkes: Director of Product Development and Manufacturing
Client:	Marshall Baby Care Products

The Royalty Stroller weighs 17 pounds and folds to the size of a traditional umbrella stroller. The 5 position reclining seat converts from fully reclined to upright seating. A clear plastic window in the retractable sun canopy allows parents to view their child in any of five positions. A fabric boot attaches to the stroller armrest surrounding the child's foot and lap area. Additional features include front swivel wheels which lock individually for easy maneuverability on rough surfaces, and a one foot lever braking system which locks all four wheels.

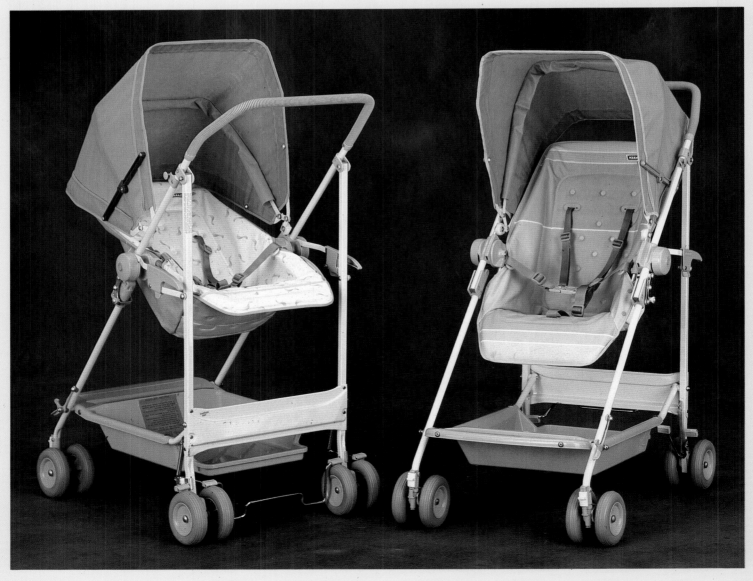

Chapter 4
Toys Educational

When user-centered principles are applied to the design process, designing for children is really no different than designing for any other target audience. User-centered design principles place the end user of the product at the center of the design process, so that all critical decisions are based upon what most appropriately addresses the end user's needs. In order to achieve effective user-centered design, it is of paramount importance that the design team be knowledgeable regarding all of the pertinent criteria relating to the end-user segment. These criteria may be anthropometric, ergonomic, cognitive/perceptual, social and/or cultural in nature.

To address the needs of children effectively, it is important for the design team to consider developmental learning principles. When information is needed, the design team will seek out appropriate data or, if such data is unavailable, create tests to obtain it. A mistake commonly made by manufacturers is to think of children simply as "little people," then scale down an adult product to "fit" a child. In fact, such a scaled-down product may "fit" anthropometrically, yet may still have a terrible cognitive "fit." The target audience, whether it be children, adults, or the aged, must first be understood before designing can begin.

—James S. Couch, *Director*
Product Design & Development
RichardsonSmith

Keith J. Kresge, *Vice President*
Exploratory Design Lab
RichardsonSmith

Elizabeth B.-N. Sanders, *Associate*
Vice President
Communication Design
RichardsonSmith

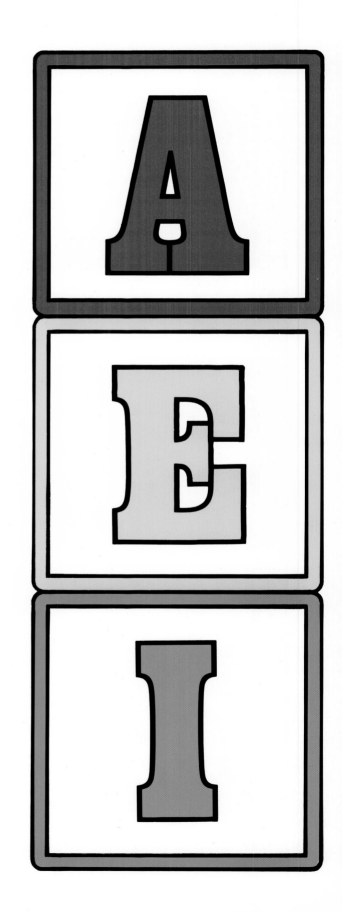

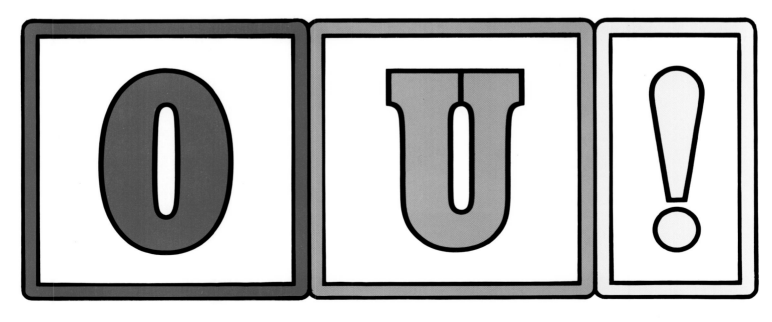

Product:	Color Frames
Design Team:	Karen Hewitt—President/ Designer
	Francis Hewitt—Artist
Client:	Learning Materials Workshop

These blocks were designed as a learning tool that would teach basic color theory (hue/value/intensity) and also provide room for experimentation and open-ended play in a simple straightforward fashion.

Forty-two different hand crafted, hardwood notched modular units are painted in forty-two different colors allowing a variety of exploratory games. Blocks can be arranged in a variety of ways to show color relationships or build imaginative structures.

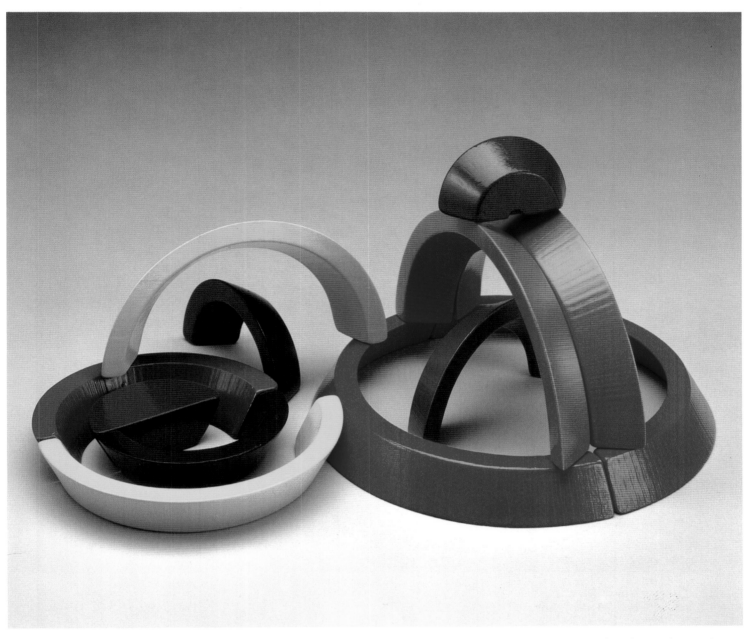

Product:	Arcobaleno
Design Team:	Karen Hewitt—President/ Designer
	Michael Delaney— Hardwood Geometrics
Client:	Learning Materials Workshop

Arcobaleno is Italian for rainbow. These colorful arches can create rainbows and much more. Beautifully crafted out of Vermont hardwoods and brightly painted in non-toxic colors they are a puzzle and a construction toy rolled into one.

Winner of the Parent's Choice Award, children can assemble the arches to form a circular puzzle or stretch their imaginations to create bridges, tunnels, bowls, domes, towers, spiral houses, sculptural forms and even a red-tailed tiger.

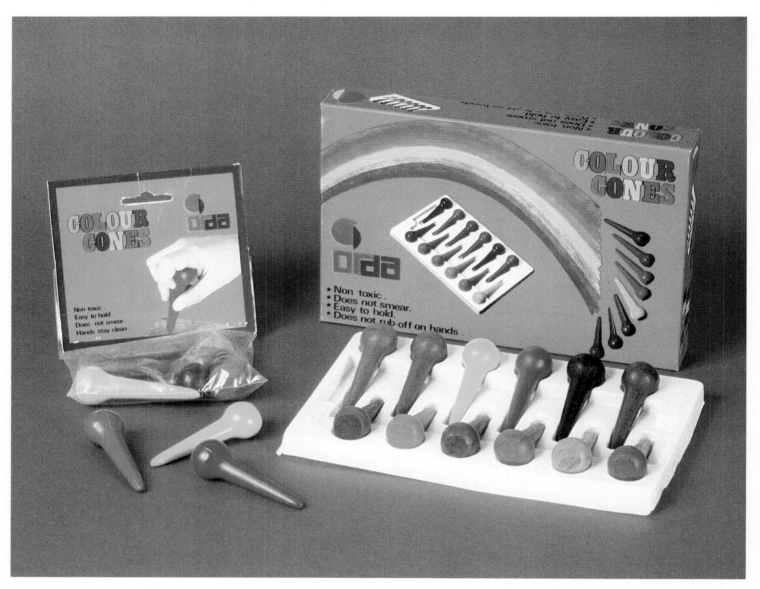

Product: Colour Cones
Design Firm: Gonis-Werke of Germany
Client: Orda Industries (USA) Inc.

These crayons are specially designed to be easy for young hands to hold and use. The non-toxic colors do not smear or rub off onto the user's hands, and are available in two different size packages.

Product: Ring-O-Links
Design Team: Uri Hirshfeld, Product Design Manager
Design Firm: Kibbutz Malkiya Orda Industries Ltd.
Client: Orda Industries (USA) Inc.

This special plastic is formed into links that are colorful, strong and flexible. Chains can be used as hanging toys for cribs or strollers to amuse infants. Older children can use the links to make chains to wear or hang in their rooms. Ring-O-Links develops dexterity, teaches color, and allows children imaginative, creative play.

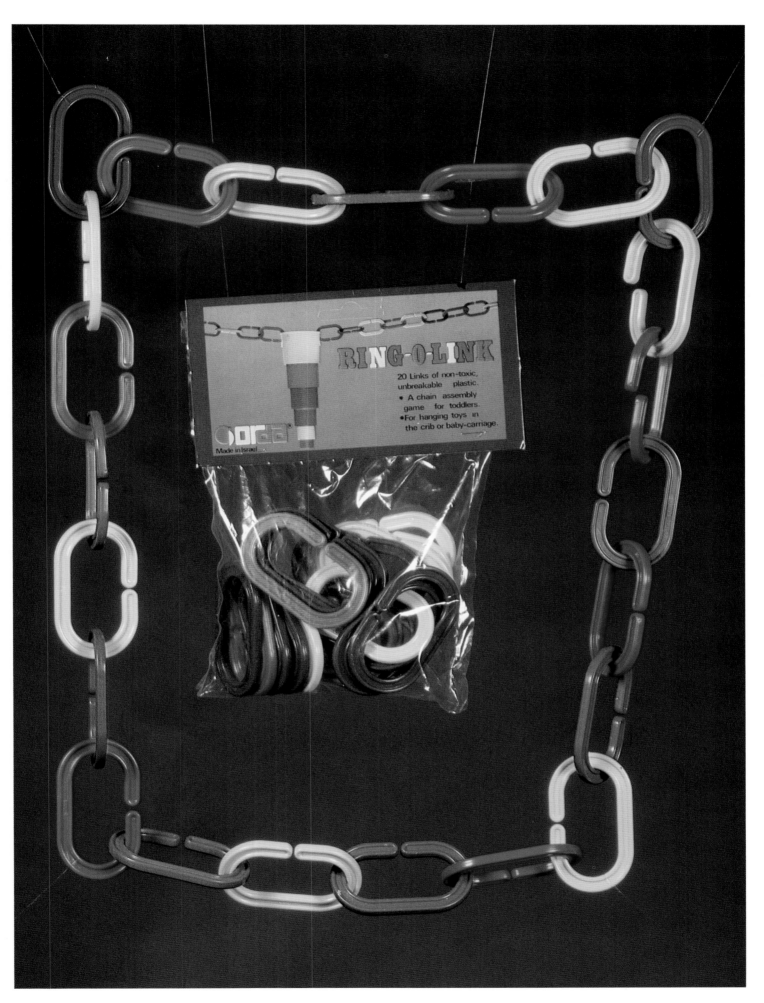

Product: Color Clowns
Design Firm: Theora Design
Client: Orda Industries (USA) Inc.

This game teaches youngsters how secondary colors are formed. The soft, see-through plastic shapes are placed over corresponding shapes on the clowns to let the child see how primary colors combine to create secondary colors. The boards are laminated for durability and hygiene.

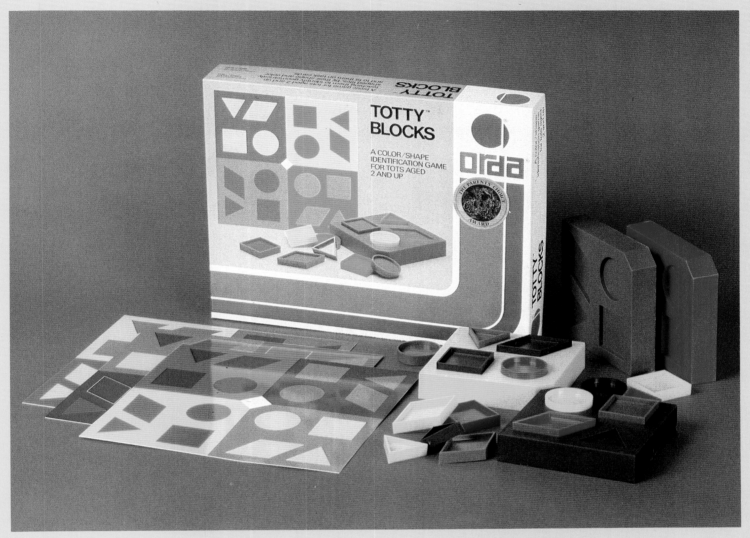

Product:	Totty™ Blocks
Design Team:	Uri Hirshfeld, Product Development
Design Firm:	Kibbutz Malkiya Orda Industries Ltd.
Client:	Orda Industries (USA) Inc.

This winner of the Parent's Choice Magazine Award is a fun way to develop a child's visual and motor skills. Totty Blocks introduces children to matching and spatial arrangement concepts. The child's manipulation of the pieces develop dexterity and coordination.

Product: Tri 3™
Design Firm: Design Associates, Orda
                  Industries Inc.
Client: Orda Industries (USA) Inc.

This three-dimensional form game teaches
a child the visual concept of form and
structure by having them match the forms
to shapes that are molded into a tray.
Since all three shapes make up the single
three-dimensional form, a child must learn
to distinguish between a circle, a square
and a triangle. The pieces come in four
different colors so the game can be played
by up to four children.

Product: Learning Curves
Design Team: Robin Kupfer, Designer
Karen Corell, Designer/
  Account Manager
Herbert M. Meyers, Design
  Supervisor
Juan Concepcion, Creative
  Supervisor
Frank Cowan, Photographer
Peter Pioppo, Photographer
Design Firm: Gerstman & Meyers, Inc.
Client: Panosh Place

Gerstman & Meyers created distinct packaging graphics for Learning Curves, Panosh Place's new line of soft, interchangeable, brilliantly-colored toys with velcro fasteners. Large, colorful product photographs and bold, red Learning Curves logo stand out against the serene gray packages, providing an impactful retail billboard.

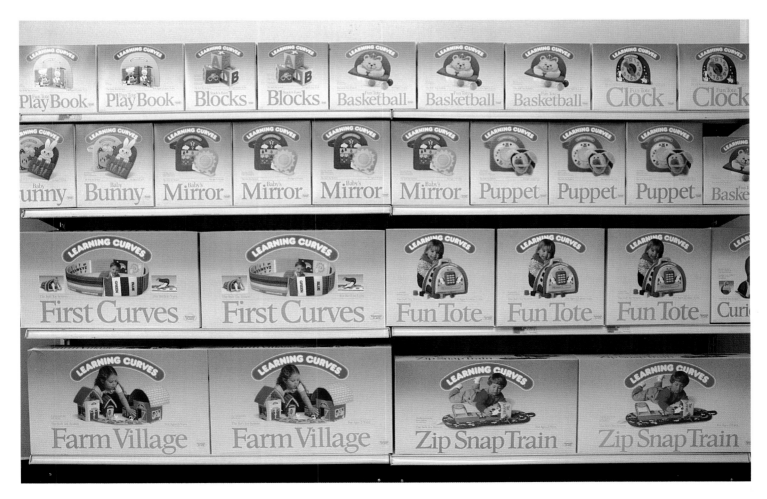

Product: Microscope
Designers: Robert P. Gersin, Design Director—Robert P. Gersin Design Associates
Client: Xerox Corporation

This simple and sturdy microscope has a visual and physical orientation that makes the mode of operation self-evident for primary school children.

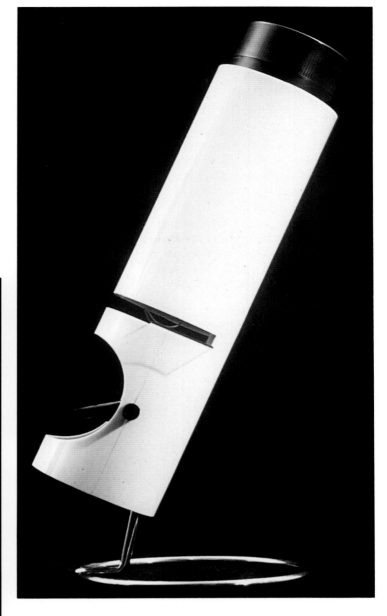

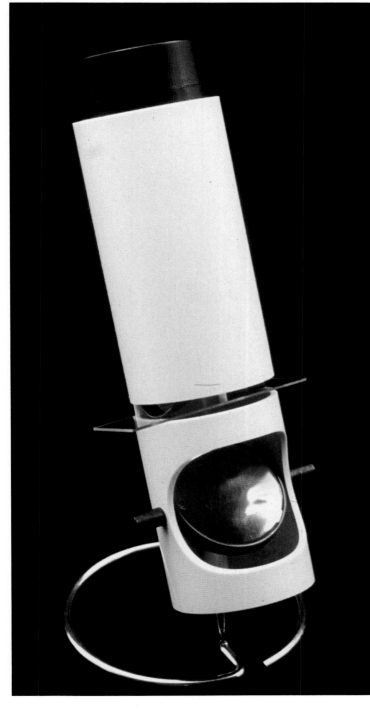

Product: The Aqua Learn Children's
Swimaid
Designer: In-House
Client: Aqua Learn Inc.

This unisex learn-to-swim aid is
lightweight, stretchy, quick drying and
puncture proof. Basically, it's a swimsuit
fitted with several individually removable
poly foam floats. This allows you to adjust
and reduce buoyancy, and the child's
dependence on it, in easy stages, as they
gain confidence in their ability to swim.
Aqua Learn allows complete freedom to
the child's arms and legs, so they can get
arms paddling and legs kicking right away.

Product:	The Bug Book and the Bug Bottle	Catching bugs is a part of every child's exploration of the world around them. With The Bug Book and The Bug Bottle this fun becomes science. The unbreakable plastic bottle has a removable lid that is perforated with air holes, so bugs can be kept and observed. The book is child-sized and has pictures and descriptions of 24 common backyard insects with facts on the insect's food and habitat as well as a glossary of insect terms.
Designer:	Susan Stirling Charles Kreloff (Art Director)	
Client:	Workman Publishing	

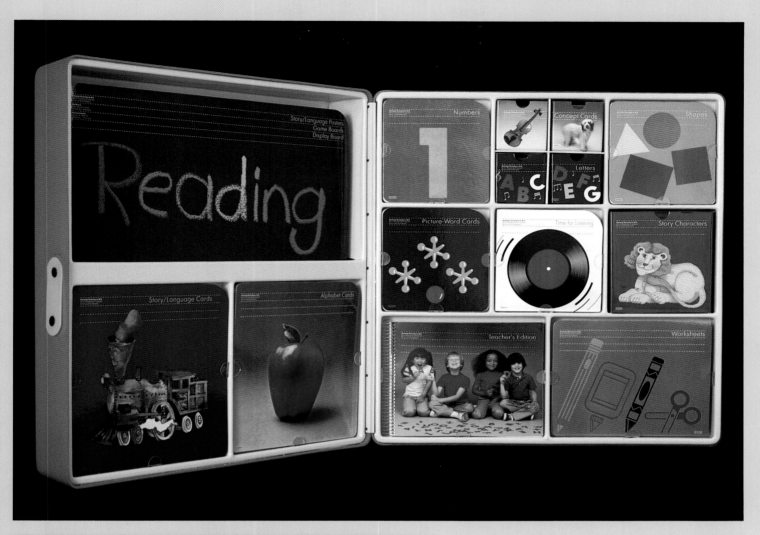

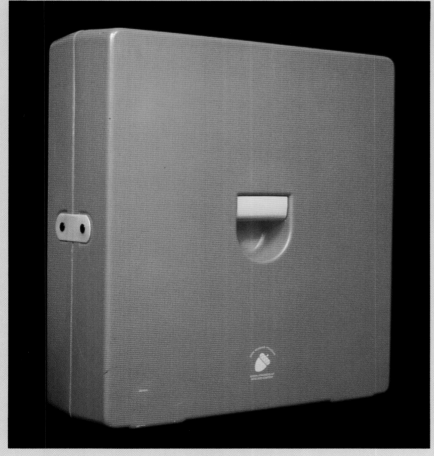

Product: Animal Crackers Reading Readiness Kit

Designers: Robert P. Gersin, Design Director; Daniel Murphy, Product Designer; David Curry, Graphic Designer—Robert P. Gersin Design Associates

Client: Ginn and Company (a Division of Xerox Corporation)

This reading kit contains a year-long set of reading readiness lessons for a kindergarten class to assist children in developing auditory and visual skills, oral language, literary comprehension, color recognition, letter recognition, number recognition, and letter/sound correspondences.

Animal Crackers Kit
Ginn Reading Program
Ginn and Company

Teacher's Edition

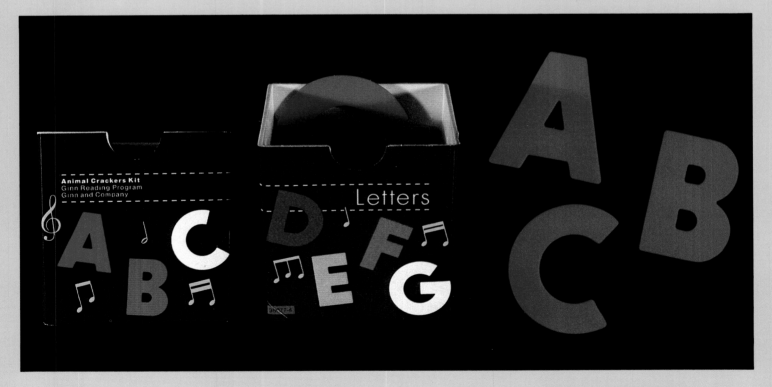

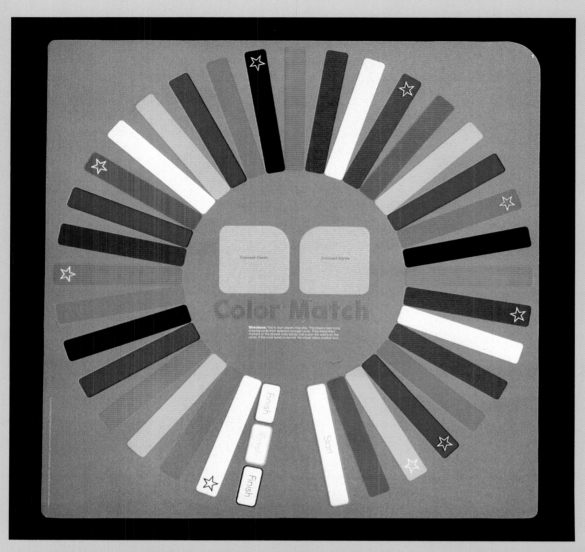

Product:	Animal Crackers Reading Readiness Kit
Designers:	Robert P. Gersin, Design Director; Daniel Murphy, Product Designer; David Curry, Graphic Designer— Robert P. Gersin Design Associates
Client:	Ginn and Company (a Division of Xerox Corporation)

This reading kit contains a year-long set of reading readiness lessons for a kindergarten class to assist children in developing auditory and visual skills, oral language, literary comprehension, color recognition, letter recognition, number recognition, and letter/sound correspondences.

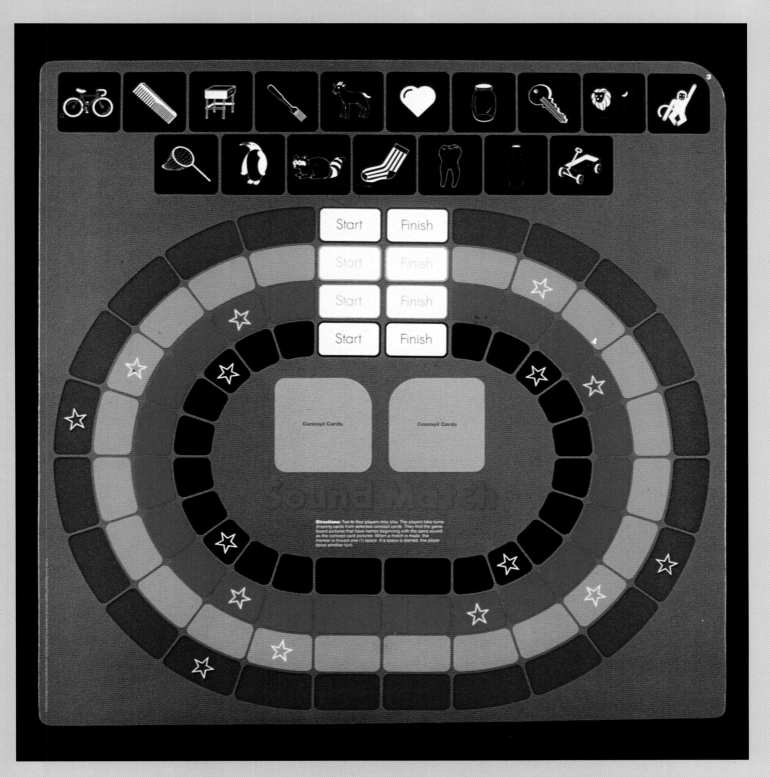

Product: Francine Sings Keepsake Series

Design Firm: Lancaster Productions— Francine Lancaster and Barbara Michaud/Kajun Graphics—Pat Koren, Laurie Smith

Client: Lancaster Productions

The Francine Sings Keepsake Series includes: Mother Goose and Other Nursery Songs, Favorite Holiday Songs, Nursery Songs and Lullabies, and Favorite Animal Songs, which is a Parents' Choice Award winner. The musical cassettes come in Dolby stereo, with full orchestral arrangements and have fanciful sound effects. The Songbooks are fully illustrated and contain 40 pages. Lyrics and music are included for each song with drawings of instruments used to teach children the various musical families.

Product: Texas Instruments Voyager

Design Team: James Couch, Director, Product Design

Deane Richardson, Co-Chairman

Keith Kresge, Vice-President, Product Design

Elizabeth B.-N. Sanders, Associate Vice President, Information Design

Scott Stropkay, Associate, Product Design

Bob Mervan, Associate, Product Design

Design Firm: Richardson Smith Inc.

Client: Texas Instruments, Inc.

The product is constructed of injection molded plastics and polyester foam. The headset is adjustable, as is the microphone. Various colors were used to appeal to children of both sexes and to identify the various parts of the headset. Many safety features were includes, such as: padding for comfort, an ear phone design that allows environmental input from the right ear, and a volume control to prevent hearing damage. All of these educational, safety, and design features earned the Voyager the 1988 ID Annual Design Review's award for Best of Category, Consumer Products.

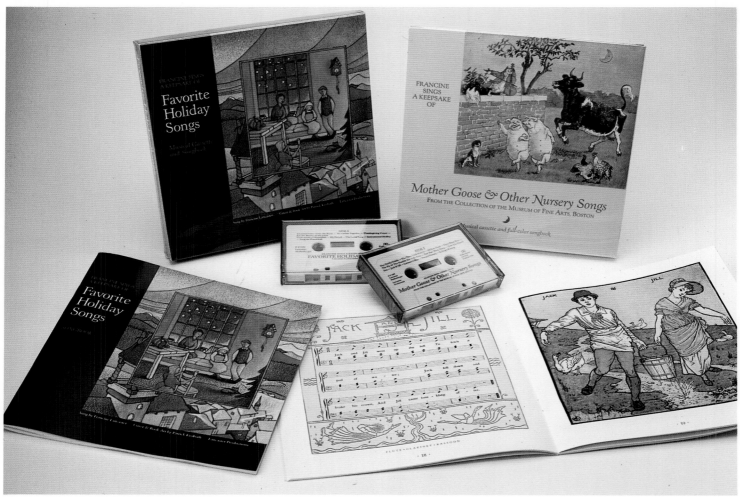

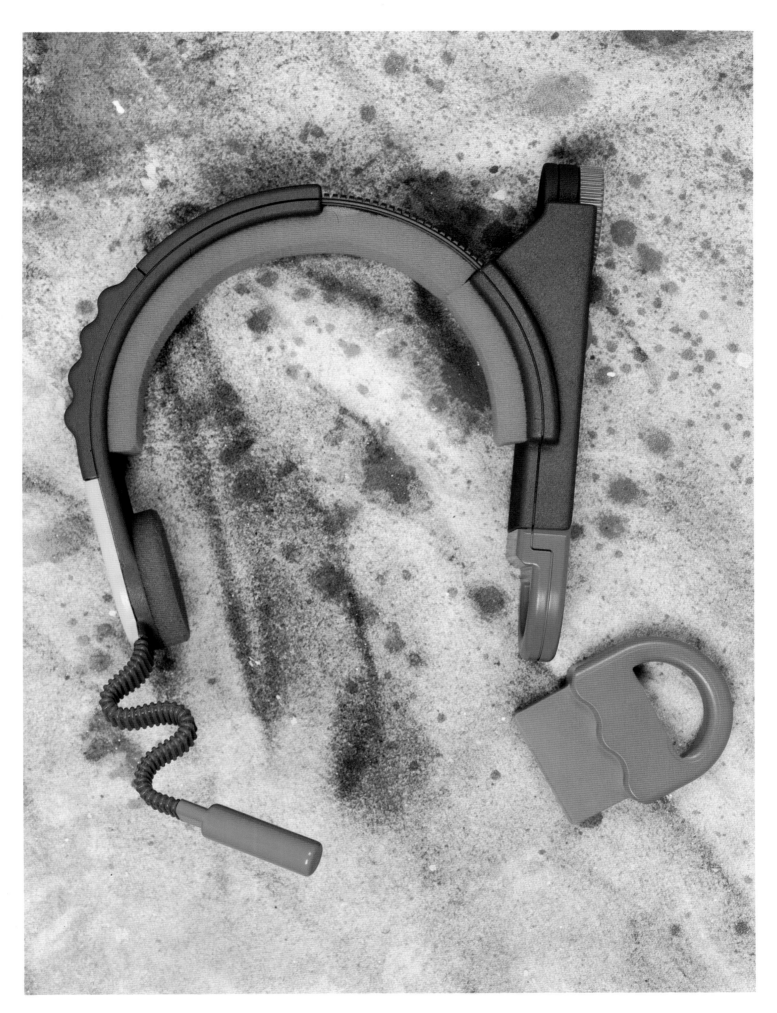

Product:	Stuffed Crib Toys
Design Firm:	Veda Incorporated
Design Team:	John Marshall, Randy Frank, Gilbert Mead
Client:	TOT Incorporated

The Stuffed Crib Toys by Turn On Toys offer stimulation and interest that eliminates crying, which is largely due to boredom. Constructed of 100 percent cotton shells and trims and non-allergenic polyester fill, these make them pleasant for babies to touch and hold.

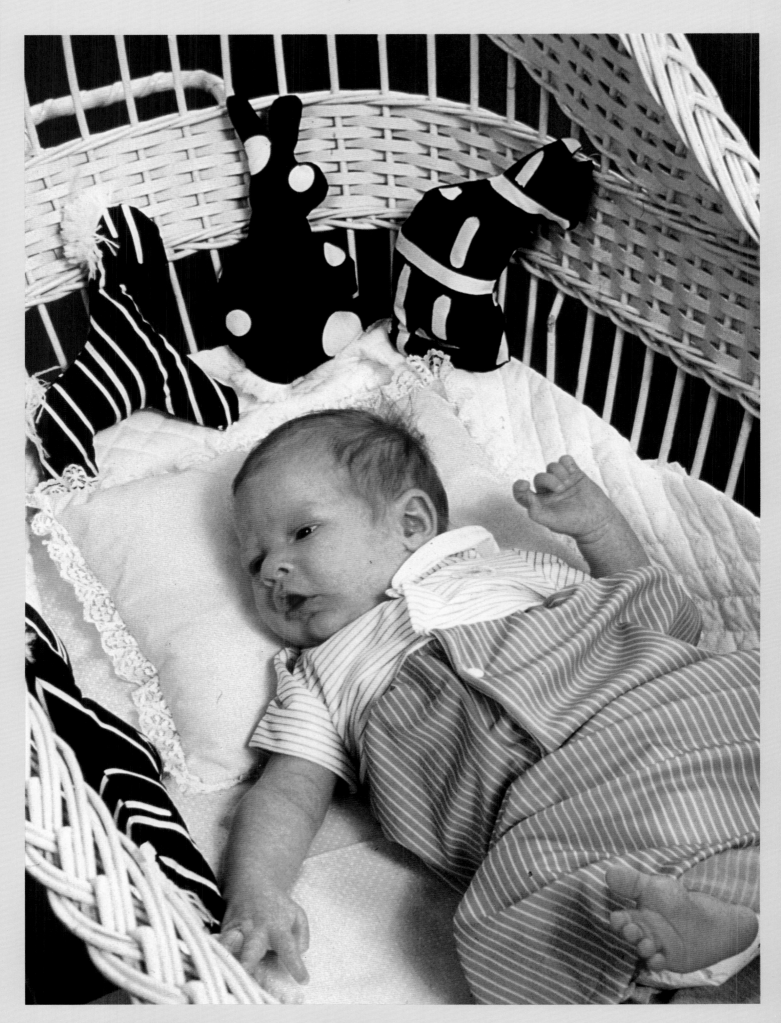

The Stuffed Crib Toys by Turn On Toys offer stimulation and interest that eliminates crying, which is largely due to boredom. Constructed of 100 percent cotton shells and trims and non-allergenic polyester fill, these make them pleasant for babies to touch and hold.

Product:	Ready...Set...Read!
Design Firm:	Texas Instruments Design Center
Client:	Texas Instruments, Incorporated

Ready...Set...Read!, a product for children three through seven years old, required a whimsical and animated appearance in tune with children today. A product which doesn't intimidate children through its technology but rather looks fun to play with and in turn fun to learn from. The toy can be opened like a book and folds into a compact portable case. It operates through activity books which are used on top of a touch sensitive pad responding to the child's touch asking questions; scoring, and rewarding while encouraging exploration.

Product: Computer Fan™
Design Firm: Texas Instruments Design Center
Client: Texas Instruments, Incorporated

Computer Fun™ is an electronic educational product designed to introduce children to computers and their capabilities. The design challenge was to develop a product which encourages imagination and exploration as well as being fun.

Looking like an adult's lap top, Computer Fun™ has a flip up screen and a real keyboard. The program choices include: make-a-word, silly stories, number play, and creature creation.

Product: Educo Super Maze
Designer: George Valentine
Client: Educo Services

Educo bead frames were designed by an educational administrator to provide opportunities for acquiring learning and manipulative skills. The colorful Super Maze provides for imaginative play in a 3-D setting. Colored wires make eye tracking easier for young children. Children of many ages and ability levels are visually attracted to the bright colors and are readily motivated to explore the differently shaped beads and wires. The wires are painted electro-statically to ensure a tough, bright, non-toxic finish, and are lodged in the wooden base by a split plastic plug that expands when the wire is inserted to keep the toy intact and prevent children from pulling the beads off the toy.

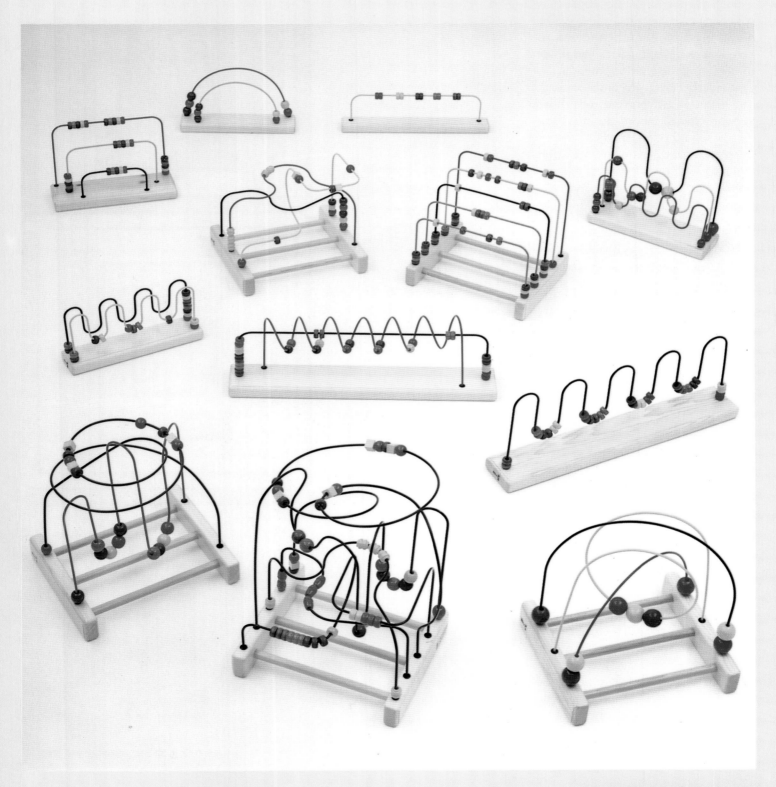

Chapter 5
Environmental

Designing for children is not unlike designing for any other audience. The designer 'role-plays' in an effort to make the design most appropriate and appealing to a specific audience. One has to put himself in the shoes of the people he's designing for. The process of designing for children then, is a particularly rewarding and pleasurable one because one can return to those things—colors, shapes, and rhythms that delighted or soothed us when we were very young—fundamental things that stay with us for the rest of our lives.

The use of large areas of primary color and simplistic shapes that allow the child to recognize and dwell on these shapes is a conscious effort to relate to how children might render the same visual concepts. Though the child's ability to recognize and deal with the composition should not be underestimated. Children can understand concepts that are quite complex if the information is staged properly, giving them the time and order necessary for them to connect the various elements. We are careful to keep the design elements simple so as not to deprive the child his right to play within the design, to close the gaps, add to or subtract from what is there. To do what children do best: use their imaginations.

The design process for us is one of indulging the child in ourselves, or an idealized remembrance of our own childhood, and what happens when that chord is struck. The magic of discovering a sphere, or cube, or a wheel for the first time. It is an exercise in which we free ourselves of most of our adult associations and judgments built up over years of becoming 'grown ups.'

—Thom Marchionna and
Rick Tharp, designers

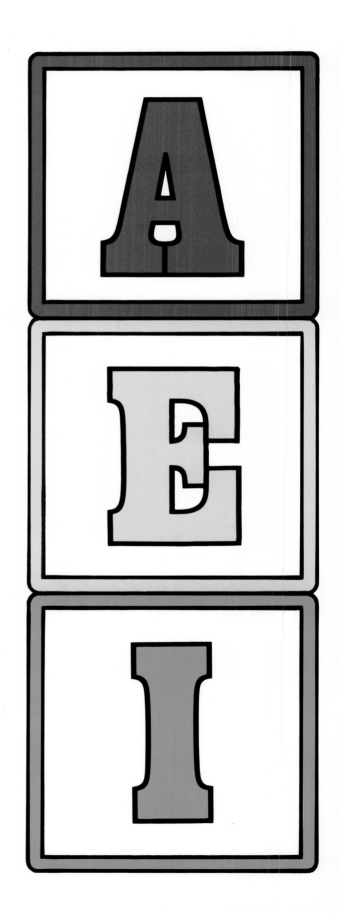

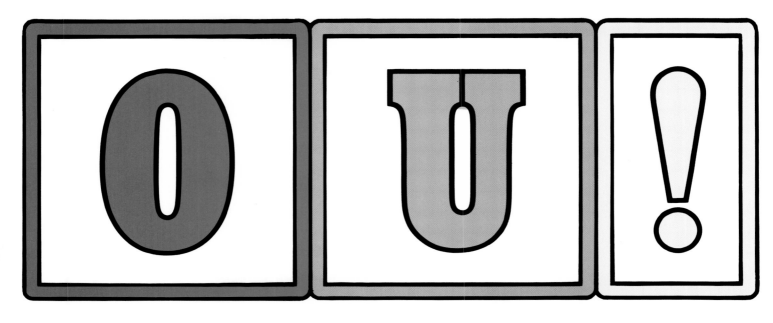

Discovery is what growing up is all about **BRIO**

Product:	Brio Poster Series
Design Firm:	Tharp Did It
Designers:	Rick Tharp and Thom Marchionna
Client:	Brio Scanditoy Corporation

The Brio Poster Series is a collection of imaginative prints focused on the world of the inquisitive child. Provocative sayings enhance each poster. For parents and children alike, these colorful prints will bring years of joy and the inspirational awareness of children to life.

To play is to learn **BRIO**

sometimes i'm happy
sometimes i'm blue
my color depends on you

Product:	Play Environment and Products
Designers:	Robert P. Gersin, Design Director; Lee H. Stout, Project Director; James Wenzel and Ingrid Caruso, Interior Designers—Robert P. Gersin Design Associates
Client:	Pediatrics Units, Brooklyn Hospital, Brooklyn, New York

The designers transformed a 180-foot corridor and play room to a delightful play and learning experience for children. They sought to provide devices that stimulate the children's sensory pleasures. The children can touch, feel, listen, observe, explore and discover. These activities help young patients to forget the unpleasant and unfamiliar surroundings of the hospital.

tic tac touch

Product: Tike™ Treehouse
Design Firm: Nottingham-Spirk Design Associates
Client: The Little Tikes Company

This rugged plastic treehouse can be used both indoors and out. With its ladder and slide it will keep active toddlers busy for hours. The bright colors and detailing make it an attractive addition to a child's playroom.

Product: Activity Gym
Design Firm: The Little Tikes Company
Client: The Little Tikes Company

This durable activity gym is constructed of sturdy polyethylene to withstand the weather and many hours of rough play. It can be used indoors or outdoors and the bright, vivid colors appeal to younger children.

Product: Playground
Designers: Robert P. Gersin, Design Director; Stephanie Kahn, Designer—Robert P. Gersin Design Associates
Client: Pearlridge Shopping Center, Pearl City, Oahu, Hawaii

This playground provides a safe, attractive play area for children in this shopping center, while resting parents can keep a watchful eye. The carpeted area contains climbing and sliding equipment, shapes and spaces to encourage imaginative play and provides open space for the children to run and be active.

Product: Signage and Wall Graphics
Designers: Bob Mervar and Keith
               Kresge, RichardsonSmith
Client: Sutter Park Elementary
               School, Worthington, Ohio

These wonderful, colorful wall graphics and signage help direct children through this Ohio elementary school, as well as teach new concepts.

Chapter 6
Clothing

A child's clothing should never interfere with the delight of being a child, and children's clothing should be designed to increase participation in this delight by the adults that love and care for the child.

Uncomfortable children get miserable and can make everyone around them miserable too. Making apparel comfortable for children however is a special challenge because children maintain a remarkable level and variety of physical activity. I approach this as an exercise in dynamic solid geometry. I begin each design by devising a garment body to suit the physical activities specific to the age range I am working with, then I structure the garment to be appropriate to the dressing skills of that age.

Once I have provided a solution for the more functional, and structural demands of a garment I use intrinsic shape and line as the basis for my styling. I feel children in these early years should be unselfconscious about their clothes and I employ understated styling to highlight their delightful natural spontaneity.

Even very young children have clear color and texture preferences and almost universally like strong clear colors and soft textures.

When I have developed a design which is comfortable and lets the child inside look their best, I consider the grown ups taking care of that child and its clothes and work with fabrics which are of excellent quality and which are easy to take care of. Naturally active spontaneous children are hard on their clothes and get very dirty.

In summary, children's clothing must: be comfortable in use and in motion; be age appropriate; allow for growth and change; wear well; and let children look like children.

—Alice Williford
American Widgeon

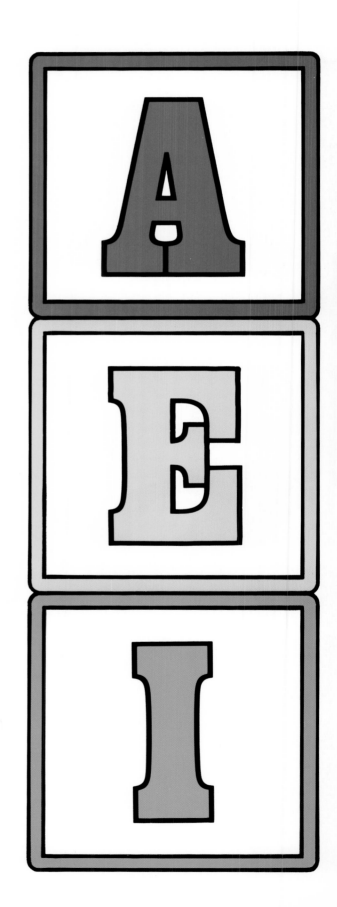

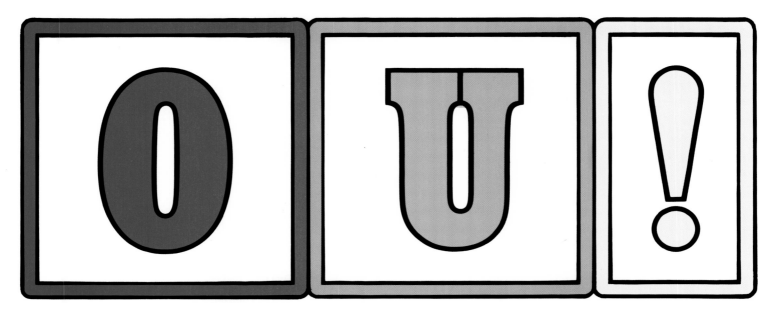

Product: Golden Rainbow Ensemble
Design Team: Natalie Mallinckrodt:
President/Mary De Yoe:
Merchandise Manager/Pearl
Chow: Merchandising
Assistant
Client: Golden Rainbow

The Golden Rainbow Dress for Girls and
Suit for Boys are designed to be both
practical and fashionable. Only the highest
quality materials available are used making
them washable and affordable.

The Golden Rainbow Ensemble is
constructed of cotton fabric with only the
highest quality materials available. The
emphasis of Golden Rainbow is high
quality, fun, sophisticated clothing for
children.

Golden Rainbow's Clothing are constructed of different fabrics with coordination patterns that create fashionable and interesting ensembles, while also being washable and affordable.

Product: Rainbow Zipper Design with
                 Charms
Designer: Sarabelle Prince
Design Firm: Prince Prints Inc.

The focal point of this dress (the design is
also available on T-shirts or sweat suits) is
a brilliantly colored rainbow of colored
zippers with charm pulls. Not only does
the child learn the colors of the rainbow,
but also can practice the manual skills
required to open and close a zipper. The
charms make the zippers easier for little
hands to use and are a source of delight for
the proud wearer.

    To make the garments easy for parents
to care for, they are made of 100 percent
preshrunk cotton and the charms can be
removed before washing. The bright colors
are colorfast non-toxic dyes; they won't
run or fade. The appliques are backed and
finished with a satin stitch so they can be
removed from the garment when the child
outgrows it and resewn on another outfit.

Product: Basic Dress
Designer: LynMarie K. Volpatti
Client: Casa Volpatti

The Casa Volpatti Basic Dress is 100 percent cotton, easy to clean, and provides the child with plenty of room for play and movement.

Product: Bubble Skirt and Blouse
Designer: LynMarie K. Volpatti
Client: Casa Volpatti

The Bubble Skirt and Blouse by Casa Volpatti leaves plenty of room for little arms and legs to stretch and move. The skirt and blouse bring back the fashions of the past vibrantly.

Product:	Warmsuit with Shell
	Widgeon Jacket
Designer:	Alice Williford
Client:	American Widgeon

The makers of this children's outerwear threw out conventional wisdom on children's sizing and outerwear bodies and developed a range approach to sizing and designed entirely new snowsuits and jackets. American Widgeon wanted to design outerwear that a child could use for at least two years during rapid growth and change in their body shape. Other concerns were making them easy to get in and out of, easy to clean and making them warm and waterproof to keep children comfortable.

The two jackets shown are both the same size yet the design features accommodate the changing shape of a child's growing body. The jacket design includes mechanical adjustments that allow the jacket to grow with the child.

Product:	WeatherSnap
Design Team:	Ginger Ardid and Jeronimo Jergins
Client:	SnipSnap Incorporated

The Weathersnap is constructed of 100 percent nylon, is water resistant and breathable. Weathersnap has a specially designed elasticized hem which wraps your child snugly into any transportation carrier. Weathersnap will grow with your children and their needs from infancy to 5 years of age.

Product:	The Rescued Robin Clothing
Designer:	Deborah Kavakos
Design Firm:	The Rescued Robin
Client:	The Rescued Robin

These clothes are made of 100 percent cotton and designed to be comfortable, convenient and fashionable. The clothing is adjustable to increase longevity of wear with two button straps, elastic waists and cuffed pant legs. To make them easier for children to manage they are roomy, have large buttons and at least one pocket for collected treasures.

The clothing is designed to be fashionable without making a pre-schooler look like a tiny teen. The cotton fabric is comfortable, durable and easy to care for. All these outfits reflect the ideal of clothing designed to celebrate childhood.

Product: Baby Bag Snowsuit
Design Firm: Baby Bag Company
Designer: Elizabeth Andrews
Client: Baby Bag Company

The unique design of The Baby Bag is all an infant will need for cool weather. In colder temperatures, a hat, sweater and mittens (or The All-In-One Warm Up Suit) give all the added protection necessary. The Baby Bag slips on and off in seconds, is ideal for carseats, strollers or carriers, adjusts quickly for temperature and diaper changes, and it's superior fabrics and sleeveless design keep cold out and warmth in.

Product: Various Clothing
Design Team: Brenda Youness—owner/
    designer
Teresa Gelson—designer
Susan Wiedenmeyer—
    designer
Client: Heart's Designs, Inc.

What better way for a child to celebrate a birthday than to wear their very own birthday cake. These colorful appliques come on a variety of outfits and the number of candles will tell the world how old the child is.

A wide variety of appliques are available on acrylic fleece for durable, comfortable, easy care garments that kids enjoy.

Product: Depot Dads Painting Smocks

Designer: Deborah Oliveira Phelan—owner/designer

Design Firm: Diaper Depot, Inc.

Finally, a painting smock that not only keeps the paint off kid's clothes but that looks good doing it. With a mock turtle neck, long sleeves with rib-knit cuffs and velcro closures the smock will keep kid's clothes paint free and is oversized to fit over layers of clothes. The big bold paint brush designs add color to the smocks.

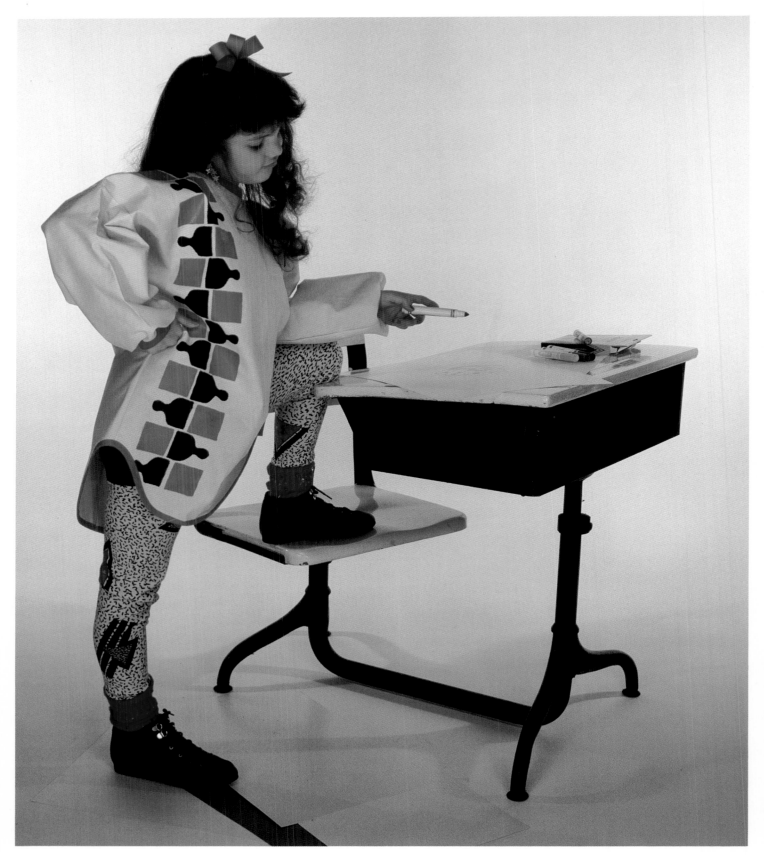

Chapter 7
Safety/Health/Food

The prenatal/postnatal market for goods and services designed for children has experienced tremendous growth in the last decade. Such growth is due partially to the growing emphasis based on providing a child with the best of everything, from strollers to schools, under the marketable premise that a well founded child will is best prepared for adulthood success.

A trip to any child's boutique, discount merchandiser or catalog showroom reveal scores of products hoping to attract volume sales with little or no attention paid to the exact purpose and part that product will play in a child's life.

—*Marshall Electronics, Inc.*

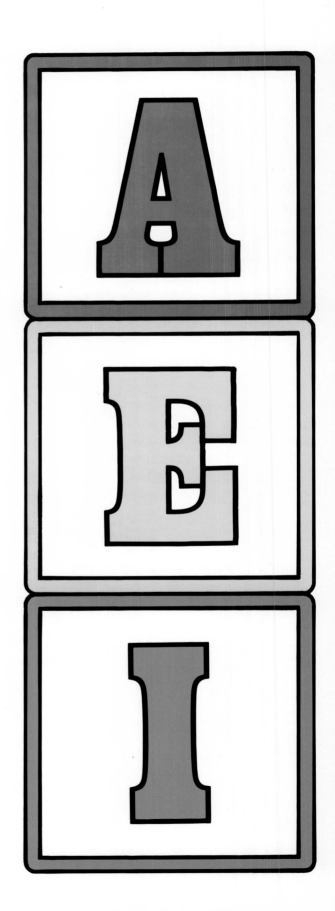

Product:	Carta-Kid
Design Firm:	The Great Kid Company
Designer:	Deborah Silke
Client:	The Great Kid Company

The Carta Kid infant and toddler seat for shopping carts meets all safety standards and hooks securely to all conventional shopping carts. The Carta Kid is color coded and folds to fit in a diaper bag. The Carta Kid is 100 percent polyester making it completely machine washable.

Product: Kid Pruf Safety Products
Design Firm: In-House

These easy to use, easy to install outlet covers offer protection against electric shock. Designed by parents to safeguard their children, they have a versatile swivel flap for quick access for vacuuming and a patented adult release lock tab.

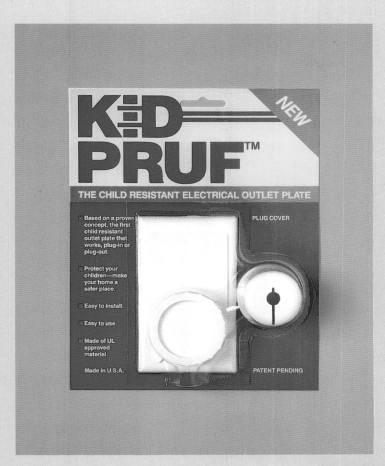

KID PRUF™

NEW

THE CHILD RESISTANT ELECTRICAL OUTLET PLATE

- Based on a proven concept, the first child resistant outlet plate that works, plug-in or plug-out.

- Protect your children—make your home a safer place.

- Easy to install.

- Easy to use.

- Made of UL approved material.

Made in U.S.A.

PLUG COVER

PATENT PENDING

Product:	Little Miss Goody Barrettes and Ponytailers Display
Design Team:	Linda R. Rothstein: Design Manager/Fred Meyer: Advertising, Display Manager
Client:	Goody Products Incorporated

Little Miss Goody Barrettes and Ponytailers Display encourage children's manual dexterity to become more focused. The thickness of materials used were tested for their strength and flexibility, keeping in mind the child's manual strength.

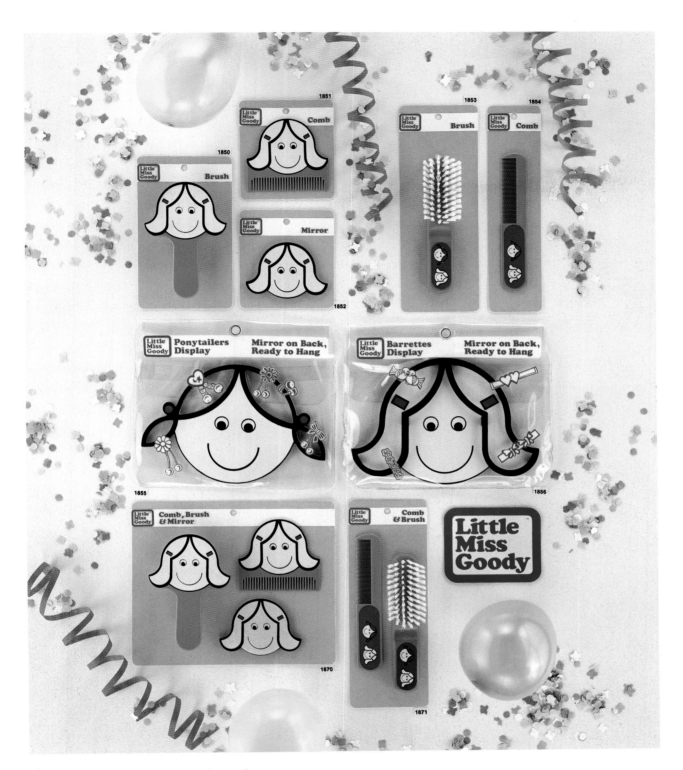

Product: Little Miss Goody Comb, Brush and Mirror Set

Design Team: Linda R. Rothstein: Design Manager/Fred Meyer: Advertising, Display Manager

Client: Goody Products Incorporated

The Little Miss Goody Comb, Brush and Mirror Set was developed for safe hair grooming, with a greater emphasis on play. The brush and comb handles are sized and shaped for children's hands. Poly bristles pattern were spaced wider apart to prevent hair from being easily tangled.

Product:	ORLAU Swivel Walker
Designer:	G.K. Rose and Engineering Team
Client:	Orlau, The Orthopedic Hospital, Owestry, Shropshire, England

Product: Children's Walker
Designer: Horst Dwinger, Rodach, West Germany
Client: Habermaass, Rodach, West Germany
Courtesy of The Able Child, New York, New York

This wooden walker allows developing toddlers the mobility they need, with the added security of support.

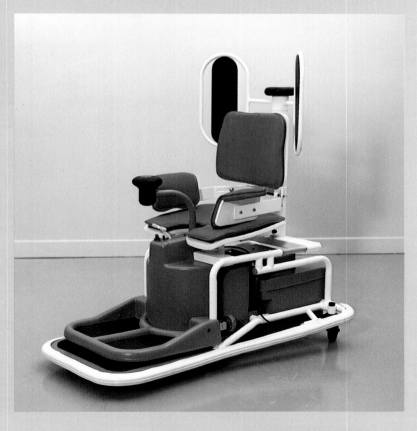

Product: Child's Wheelchair
Design Firm: Douglass Ball, Inc.

This chair comes with an adjustable seat and back and arm rest supports.

Product: Super Sunyard
Design Firm: North States Industries Incorporated
Client: North States Industries Incorporated

The Super Sunyard creates a shaded portable play area for young children. The Super Sunyard is durable, convenient and versatile, while also being washable and easy to clean. There are ground stakes included to hold the Super Sunyard securely even in wind.

Product: Superyard
Design Firm: North States Industries
Incorporated
Client: North States Industries
Incorporated

The Adjustable Size Superyard portable play area is durable, convenient and versatile. It features an expandable panel system that allows you to easily change the shape and size of the play area. The 6 interlocking panels enclose up to 8.5 square feet.

Product: Supergate
Design Firm: North States Industries
     Incorporated
Client: North States Industries
     Incorporated

North States Mesh Gates come in two
models; natural wood, and/or non-toxic
lead free clear varnish finish. The positive
tab locking hinge with safety clasp will be
durable and reliable, but most importantly,
safe.

KID'S STUFF

BREAKFAST

The Cabbage Patch
Choice of hot or cold cereal with a slice of buttered toast and preserves.

Humpty Dumpty
One egg, any style, with crisp bacon and a slice of buttered toast and preserves.

Pac-Man Cakes
Two buttermilk pancakes with cinnamon honey/butter and warm maple syrup.

Frenchies
Our special French Toast with powdered sugar and maple syrup.

CHILDREN'S FARE

Charley the Tuna $2.50
A tuna fish sandwich on white bread served with potato chips

Chicken Little $3.50
Tender fingers of white breast meat breaded and deep fried.

Dennis the Menace $1.75
Peanut Butter and Jelly sandwich on white bread served with potato chips.

Miss Piggy $2.50
Cold ham and cheese sandwich on white bread with potato chips.

The E.T. $1.95
A grilled cheese sandwich with ham and potato chips.

The Porky Pig $2.25
A hot dog and bun served with french fries.

Wimpy's Burger $2.95
A burger served plain or with American cheese and french fries.
Choice of Chilled Juice, Milk or Soda $.75

The Rainbow Connection $.95
A bowl of orange, raspberry and lime sherbet.

DESSERT

Candy's Clown $1.50
A clown made of vanilla ice cream, ice cream cone, M&M's and whipped cream.

Bullwinkie Pudding $.95
Creamy Chocolate Moose

Embassy Suites™ Hotel 888 Chesterbrook Blvd., Wayne, PA 19087. Operated by the Beacon Hotel Corporation, a member of the Beacon Companies and Embassy Suites, Inc.

Product: Menu
Restaurant: Ambassador Grille
Location: Embassy Suites Hotel, Wayne, Pennsylvania
Designer: Maura Harnagy, Art Group, Inc.
Illustrator: Al Himes

The restaurant is contemporary, but the hotel is located in the Valley Forge area. The children's menu is therefore theoretically correct for the area and its associations with George Washington. The menu has perforations that permit the child to wear the menu as a Revolutionary War era general's hat, complete with powdered wig at the back. The copywriting is quite contemporary, drawing on movies, cartoons, and current children's toy and games for the item names and associations.

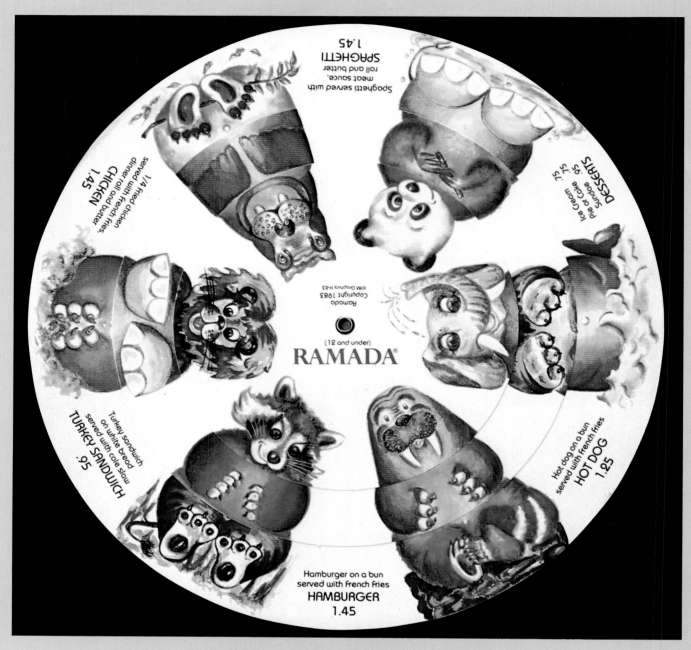

Product:	Menu
Restaurant:	Ramada Inns, Inc.
Location:	Phoenix, Arizona
Designer:	Robert Lansdell

This menu won second place in the "Specialty" category of the National Restaurant Association's 1986 Great Menus Contest. Fancifully colored animals can be reassembled at will by turning the three disks to align one animal's head with another's body and a third's feet. Since each cut in the menu is made at a point where the outlines match exactly, the game is even more fun. Some variations of the "mix and match" game have been played by children for many years, yet the game never loses its excitement. Menu items are described simply on the outermost disk. This menu provides the perfect excuse to read the menu upside down—and get away with it. The animals' faces are drawn with appealing artistry.

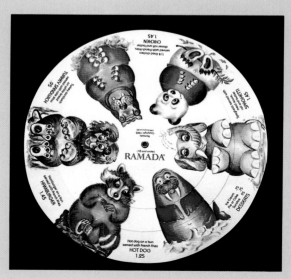

Product: Menu
Restaurant: McHenry's
Location: Sheraton Harbor Hotel,
Baltimore, Maryland
Designers: Paul Harnagy, Jeff Metzler,
Art Group, Inc.
Illustrator: Al Hines

The restaurant is named for Fort McHenry but is not colonial in theme. The coonskin cap is just a fun device for the child. In designing children's menus, thematic consistency is less important than it is for adults. If the child is entertained by an idea, that is sufficient.

McHenry's
CHILDREN'S MENU
For Children under 12

Sandwiches

Grilled Cheese Sandwich	$1.95
Hamburger/Cheeseburger	$2.25
Hot Dog	$1.50
Peanut Butter n' Jelly	$1.95

Hot Entrees

Fried Chicken	$3.75
Fried Shrimp	$4.25
Spaghetti with Tomato Sauce	$3.25
Mini Pepperoni Pizza	$4.00

Ice Cream	$1.50

Sheraton
Inner Harbor
Hotel

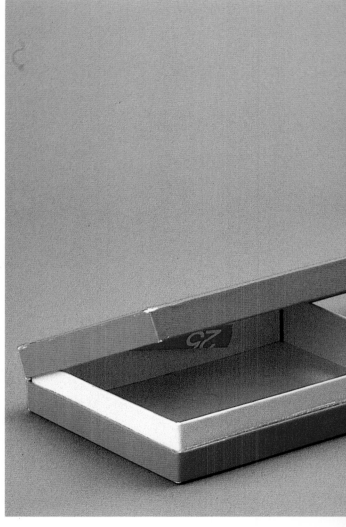

Product:	Menu
Restaurant:	Eat 'n Park Restaurants, Inc.
Location:	Pittsburgh, Pennsylvania
Designer:	Kensington Falls, Family Communications, Inc.

These little books use simple illustrations of the selections available to children, with a brief description and price (for the parents' benefit) next to the spine. Each item in the meal is depicted, and a partially consumed glass of milk is suggestively placed alongside. At the front and back are "flip sections" that simulate animation. If the book is turned over, a complete "flip story" is available for the child's amusement. The picture menu is an effective way to involve the child in planning his own meals. Nobody needs to read the words to him—he can choose, all by himself.

Product:	Menu
Restaurant:	Holiday Inns, Inc.
Location:	Memphis, Tennessee

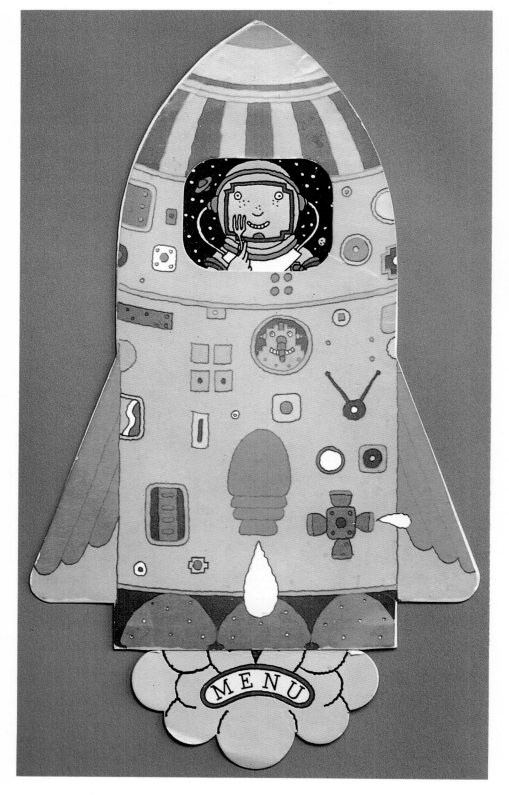

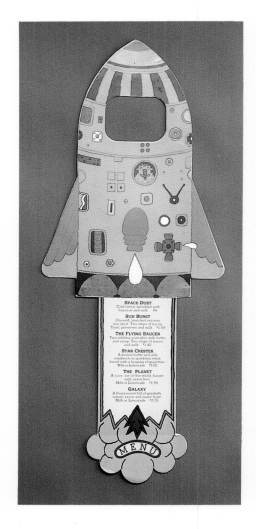

The grinning astronaut and his fork disappear as the rocket's vapor trail is pulled down to reveal the menu. Tabs concealed just below the astronaut prevent the child from pulling the menu all the way out. This probably saves quite a few menus from early destruction. The spaceship theme is carried out in the copywriting. The body of the spaceship features happy aliens concealed amid the circuitry.

Product: Menu
Restaurant: T.G.I. Friday's
Location: Nationwide chain
                         headquartered in Dallas,
                         Texas
Designer: Mike Schroeder, Pirtle
                         Design

T.G.I. Friday's shows it knows its market with this durable ringbound menu of heavy insert-card stock, printed in bright primary colors. This menu is designed to help a child practice reading skills while waiting for the meal. Large letters of the alphabet can begin to introduce capital and lowercase letters to very young children, while older children can attempt to read, or even order their own meals, depending on their reading skills. Brightly crayoned, childlike drawings depict each entry, along with simply written descriptions.

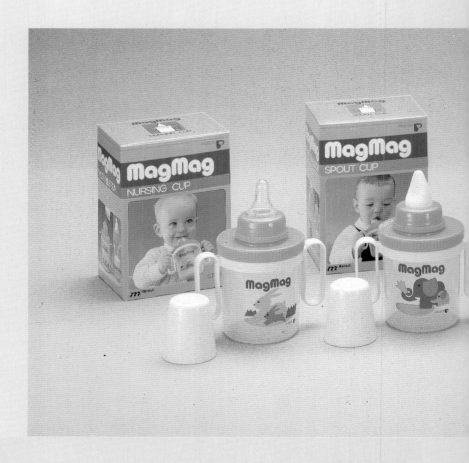

Product: Ansa Easy-To-Hold Nurser
Designer: William O. Campbell
                     Nickie G. Campbell
Client: Ansa Bottle Company, Inc.

These unique looking bottles are part of
the Museum of Modern Art's design for
Independent Living Exhibit. Their
distinctive design makes it easier to hold
them while feeding an infant, as well as
making them easier for children to handle.

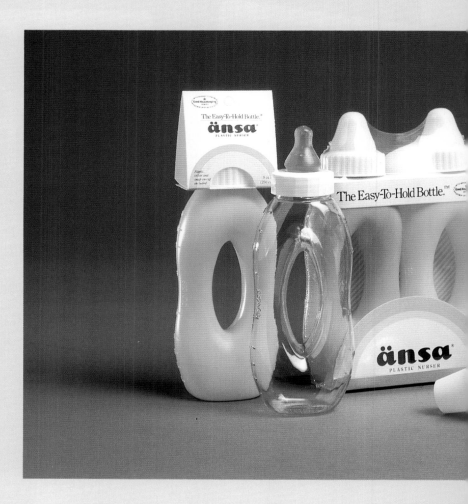

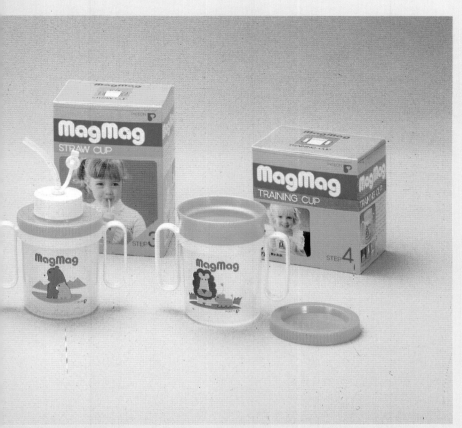

Product: MagMag Training Cup System

Design Team: Marshall Baby Care and Pigeon Corporation

Client: Marshall Baby Care Products

The MagMag Training Cup System was designed to grow with a baby from birth to 3 years of age. The Cup System trains children how to drink from either a straw or cup. The vessel is easy to hold, clean, unbreakable, and keeps liquids hot or cold.

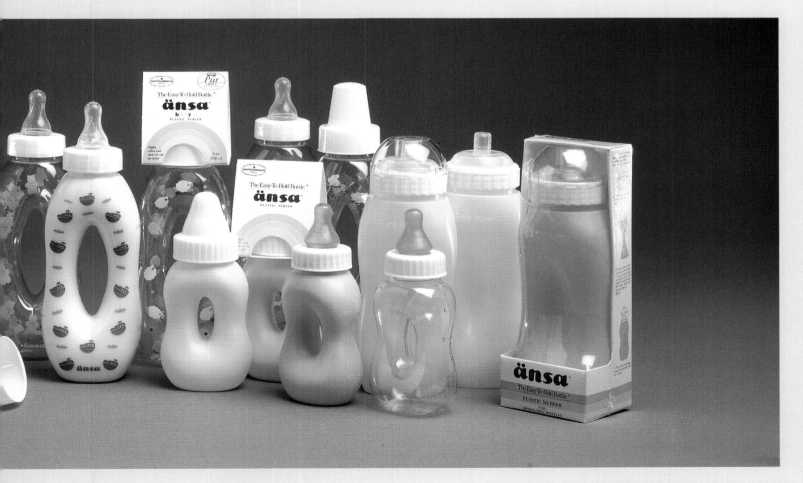

Product:	MagMag Orthodontic Training System
Design Team:	Marshall Baby Care and Pigeon Corporation
Client:	Marshall Baby Care Products

The MagMag Orthodontic Training Systems create a complete orthodontic system that helps a child's natural development of gum and tooth growth. The special teethers exercise gums while soothing sore gums and the toothbrush is used from the time of first teeth to complete set.

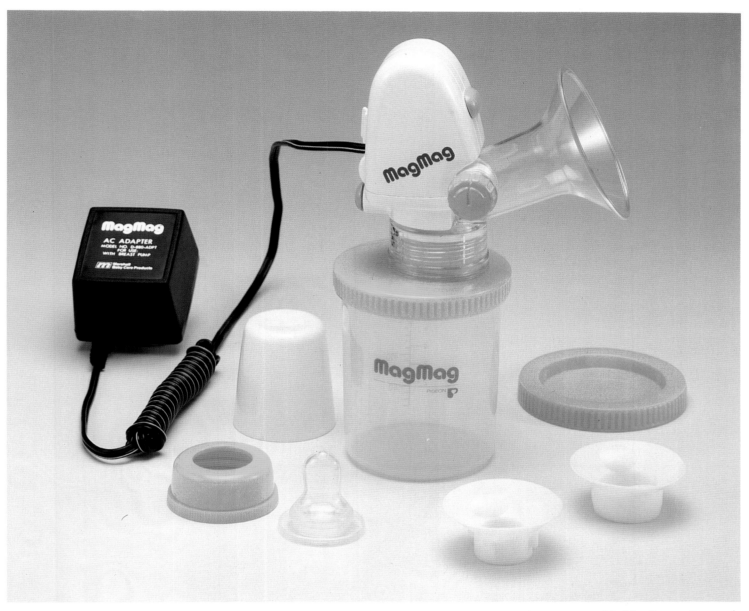

Product: MagMag Battery Operated Breast Pump with AC Adapter

Design Team: Marshall Baby Care and Pigeon Corporation

Client: Marshall Baby Care Products

The MagMag Battery Operated Breast Pump with AC adapter is the first truly portable breast pump offering single hand operation using AC electric current or batteries. The nipple adapters imitate a nursing child's natural stimulation of the milk glands and protect sore breast tissue during expression.

Product:	Crispy Critters Cereal
Designer:	Robert Wallace, Creative Director
	Stan Church, Creative Director
	Phyllis Cham, Senior Designer
Design Firm:	Wallace Church Associates
Client:	General Foods Corporation

The challenge here was to design a cereal package that would appeal to children, and communicate the product's nutritional value to parents. In order to combine the somewhat conflicting messages of a fun, good tasting cereal and a low sugar, high nutrition cereal the spokes character while being cute fun for the kids is drawn in earth tones on a sophisticated graduated grey background for the adult consumer

The back panels contain a series of fun-filled, educational games on the same graduated background which preserves the overall design integrity.

Product: Airplane Eating Tray
Design Firm: Peco
Designers: Paul Wong, Cindy Deng
Client: Peco

The Airplane Eating Tray was designed with children's imaginative curiosity in mind. Constructed with ABS plastic, Airplane Eating Tray is durable, dishwasher safe and safe for children to use.

Index

Clients

Designers

Design Firms

Illustrators

Clients

Designers

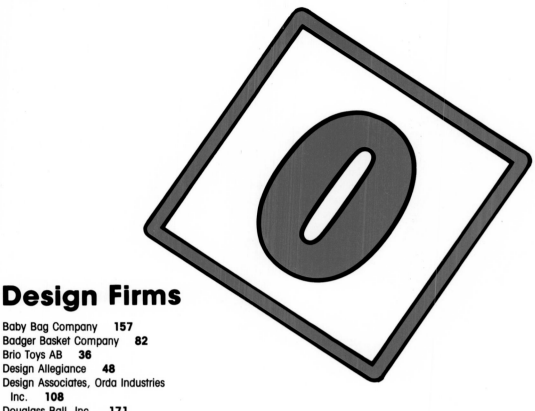

Design Firms

Illustrators